Modern American English

Robert J. Dixson
As Revised by Eugene J. Hall

2

New Edition

REGENTS/PRENTICE HALL, Englewood Cliffs, New Jersey 07632

SO-BNE-750

Library of Congress Cataloging-in-Publication Data

Dixson, Robert James.
    Modern American English 2 / Robert J. Dixson. — New ed. / rev. by
Eugene J. Hall
      ISBN 0-13-593955-0
      1. English language—Textbooks for foreign speakers.   2. English
language—Grammar—1950–   3. English language—United States.
I. Hall, Eugene J.   II. Title.
PE1128.D516 1992
428.2'4—dc20   91–12677
                                     CIP

Publisher: Tina B. Carver
Manager of Product Development: Mary Vaughn
Senior Development Editor: Nancy L. Leonhardt
Senior Production Editor: Tunde A. Dewey
Interior design and page layout: Function Through Form
Design supervision: Janet Schmid and Chris Wolf
Pre-press buyer: Ray Keating
Manufacturing buyer: Lori Bulwin

Cover design: Bruce Kenselaar
Cover photograph: © John Kelly/The Image Bank

Illustrations by Anna Veltfort

© 1992 by R. J. Dixson Associates

All rights reserved. No part of this book may be
reproduced, in any form or by any means,
without permission in writing from the publisher.

Printed in the United States of America

10

ISBN 0-13-593955-0

Contents

Preface

Modern American English 2 is the second of a series of six texts, with correlated workbooks and cassettes, designed as a complete course of study in English as a second language. The first two books provide elementary vocabulary and lay the foundations for a comprehension of the principles of English grammar; taken together, they can be considered to comprise a beginning course in English. The remaining books, the workbooks, and the cassettes build upon this foundation by expanding the study of vocabulary and completing the survey of English grammatical structures. Student book 6, although primarily a reader, provides a general review and additional practice on all the material previously studied.

The six books of the series have been planned for use in the junior high school, high school, or adult course of study. The pace of the books is measured but intensive, as is proper for students studying English on this level. Extensive oral practice is provided for everything presented. Students are prepared to move, without difficulty or confusion, from one step to the next, from one lesson to the following lesson. Vocabulary and grammar are controlled at all times, particularly at the beginning and intermediate levels in books 1 through 4. Consequently, there is no danger of teaching more vocabulary or structure than a student can readily absorb.

Expressed in a different way, the purpose of this book, as well as of the remaining books of the series, is to teach students how to use and understand spoken English. The approach emphasizes at all times the ability of the students to use what they have studied. All materials and all activities in the series contribute directly to this end.

Modern American English 2 is simple to use and easy to follow. It is a basic book, consisting of fifteen lessons. Every fifth lesson is a review that provides additional practice on the material covered in the previous four lessons. Each of the remaining lessons is divided into four sections: *Reading and Oral Practice; Structure and Pattern Practice; Pronunciation and Intonation Practice;* and *General Practice.* Each of these sections is intended to give a particular kind of practice that will strengthen the students' learning experience and lead to their ability to communicate in the new language.

1. Reading and Oral Practice. This section introduces the material that is to be studied in the lesson. It usually consists of a series of questions and answers cued to pictures. This introductory material is usually connected into a brief narrative. Most of the lessons present both structural material—verb tenses, possessive forms, and so on— and cultural material—addresses, directions, articles of clothing, colors, and so on. In addition, short dialogues introduce the students to the conversational uses of the structural patterns they have been studying. Notes on idiomatic and cultural material are introduced at the end of the section in which such expressions are first used.

The first part of each section is intended primarily for listening and repeating practice. That is, the students should listen while the teacher reads the sentences; then the students should repeat them in chorus after the teacher; third, individual students should be asked to repeat both questions and answers; and finally, individual students should read the sentences, both questions and answers.

In the next section, the students answer questions based on the previous material that are cued to the same or similar pictures. The teacher should first go over this section as a listening practice, giving both questions and answers; choral and individual repetition should follow; then the teacher should ask the questions while individual students give the answers. As a final step, one student asks the questions and another student gives the answers. This kind of student-student practice is highly recommended for all the exercises throughout the book.

In general, the structural and cultural material is presented separately but in the same manner—that is, with a listen and repeat practice first and a question and answer practice second.

Similar procedures should be followed for the dialogues—listening, choral and individual repetition, teacher-student practice, and student-student practice.

2. Structure and Pattern Practice. This section is devoted to the study of grammatical structures and patterns in English. First, explanatory notes on the structure or structures are presented in the lesson. Each note is followed by one or more exercises to give the students practice on the pattern discussed in the preceding note. The exercises are intended to help the students achieve command of the formal features of English.

It is suggested that the teacher first go through each exercise orally, with students repeating each cue and its answer in chorus. In the next step, the teacher should present the cue and then ask the class to give the answer in chorus. After that, the teacher should give the cue, with individual students giving the answer. Wrong answers should be corrected immediately with the right ones, which the students should then repeat in chorus.

When sufficient oral work has been done, the teacher can assign the exercises as written homework. Homework should be corrected carefully and returned to the students so that they can note their errors and observe their progress. The exercises in this section are designed for habit formation on specific patterns, whereas the conversation practice in the final section of the lesson is designed to give the students greater flexibility in the *use* of the patterns.

3. Pronunciation and Intonation Practice. This section gives practice on different aspects of pronunciation. In this particular book, each lesson contains minimal pair drills on contrasted vowel sounds. Many words are given in these drills that are *not* intended for vocabulary study, but *only* for pronunciation practice. For intonation practice, special exercises are marked with intonation patterns.

The material in this section should be presented by means of choral and individual repetition. The teacher's pronunciation and intonation will serve as a model for the students. The sentences for intonation practice should be said at a natural conversational speed so that the students will become accustomed to the sound of English as it is actually spoken. The cassettes give valuable additional practice for this section.

4. General Practice. This section gives oral practice in the actual use of English for conversational purposes. Several of the exercises are question and answer practices based on the material presented previously in the lesson. The questions are cued to visual information for which verbal equivalents are to be given. Procedures should consist first of teacher-student practice, in which the teacher asks the questions and individual students respond. Second should be student-student practice, in which one student acts as teacher and another makes the appropriate responses.

All of the lessons include a controlled conversation practice. Questions are given which the students can answer from their own experience and knowledge within the structural and cultural framework of the patterns and vocabulary that have been studied. These exercises are only suggestions. Each teacher should work out the particular exercise, with appropriate questions and commands, before giving it to the students, so that it will conform to the reality of that particular classroom and group of students.

SUPPLEMENTARY MATERIAL. A Teacher's Edition is available for each level of this series. For each book, a companion workbook is available in which each workbook lesson is closely coordinated with the corresponding lesson in its matching book. The workbooks provide additional material to help build all four of the language skills: listening, speaking, reading, and writing. For even more oral practice, cassettes may be obtained that cover the material in each of the book lessons.

Reading and Oral Practice

A. Listen and repeat.

What kind of building is this?
It's an apartment building.

Is it a long way from downtown?
No, it's near downtown.

Who lives here?
Joan Rossi lives here.

Where does she work?
She works in Dick's office.

What does she do?
She's the manager's assistant.

What does Dick do?
He's the mail clerk.

Who is Tony Martinez?
He's Dick's friend.

How did Tony and Dick get to know each other?
They're in the same computer class.

What did Tony do last week?
He moved into Joan's building last week.

What time is it now?
It's half past eight now.

Where is Tony?
He's at the bus stop.

Who else is there?
Joan is there too.

> *Downtown* refers to the central business and commercial district of a city or town.
>
> *There* is used as an adverb of place as well as a substitute subject. *Here* indicates a place near the speaker, and *there* indicates a place at a distance from the speaker.

B. Answer the questions.

1. What kind of building is this?

2. Is it a long way from downtown?

3. Who lives here?

4. Where does she work?

5. What does she do?

6. What does Dick do?

7. Who is Tony Martinez?

8. How did Tony and Dick get to know each other?

9. What did Tony do last week?

10. What time is it now?

11. Where is Tony?

12. Who else is there?

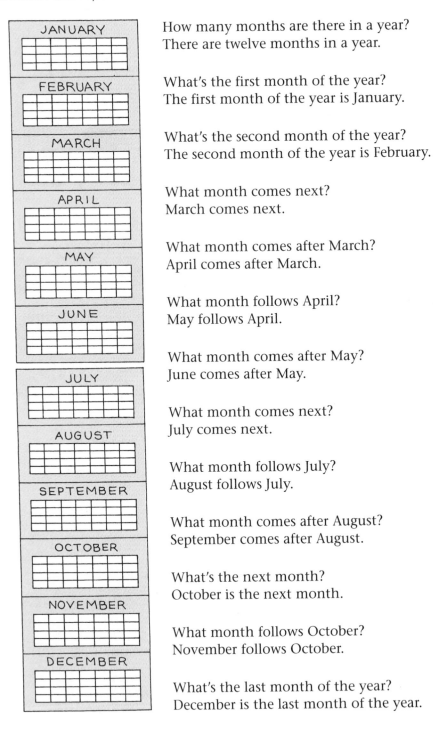

How many months are there in a year?
There are twelve months in a year.

What's the first month of the year?
The first month of the year is January.

What's the second month of the year?
The second month of the year is February.

What month comes next?
March comes next.

What month comes after March?
April comes after March.

What month follows April?
May follows April.

What month comes after May?
June comes after May.

What month comes next?
July comes next.

What month follows July?
August follows July.

What month comes after August?
September comes after August.

What's the next month?
October is the next month.

What month follows October?
November follows October.

What's the last month of the year?
December is the last month of the year.

D. Answer the questions.

JANUARY	FEBRUARY	MARCH	APRIL
MAY	JUNE	JULY	AUGUST
SEPTEMBER	OCTOBER	NOVEMBER	DECEMBER

1. How many months are there in a year?
2. What's the first month of the year?
3. What's the second month of the year?
4. What month comes next?
5. What month comes after March?
6. What month follows April?
7. What month comes after May?
8. What month comes next?
9. What month follows July?
10. What month comes after August?
11. What's the next month?
12. What month follows October?
13. What's the last month of the year?

JOAN: I met your friend this morning.

DICK: My friend?

JOAN: Tony Martinez.

DICK: Oh, Tony! Yes, he's in my computer class.

JOAN: He moved into my building last week. I met him at the bus stop this morning.

DICK: He's a nice guy.

JOAN: Is he a good student?

DICK: Yes, very good. He and I are at the top of the class.

JOAN: Is he from around here?

DICK: No, he's from Houston. He moved here last year.

JOAN: Does he have a job?

DICK: Yes, with an insurance company. His office is right over there across the street.

JOAN: He's very good-looking.

DICK: Good-looking? Do you want a date with him?

JOAN: Well, . . . maybe.

Met is the past tense form of the irregular verb *to meet*.

He meets a lot of people at school.
She met Tony at the bus stop yesterday morning.

Structure and Pattern Practice

The verb *to be* has more forms than any other verb in English. In the present the forms are:

Long Form

I am . . .   We are . . .
You are . . .   You are . . .
He is . . . ⎫
She is . . . ⎬   They are . . .
It is . . .   ⎭

Contracted Form

I'm . . .   We're . . .
You're . . .   You're . . .
He's . . . ⎫
She's . . . ⎬   They're . . .
It's . . .   ⎭

The contracted forms are generally used in conversation.

Questions are formed by placing *is, am,* or *are* before the subject.

Is Mr. Wilson in his office now?
Are they at their desks?

A. Change to questions.

EXAMPLE

The bus is green.   *Is the bus green?*

1. Tony is at the bus stop now.
2. His assistant is in the office.
3. Dick is a mail clerk.
4. Susan is late this morning.
5. The stamps are in the top drawer.
6. The envelopes are in the middle drawer.
7. Ms. Williams is a lawyer.
8. January is the first month of the year.
9. It's ten o'clock.
10. He's at school now.

> Negatives in the present tense of *to be* are formed
> by placing *not* after *is, am,* or *are.*
>
> I'm not late this morning.
> She's not at school today.

B. Change to the negative.

EXAMPLE

He's in his office.   *He's not in his office.*

1. They're at their desks.
2. We're at school.
3. She's at the hospital.
4. It's midnight.
5. I'm late this morning.
6. You're early this morning.
7. He's a salesclerk.
8. The paper is in the top drawer.
9. The magazines are on the table.
10. Dr. Stern is a teacher.

> The possessive adjectives in English always agree
> with the possessor, not with the thing possessed.
>
> I – my   he – his   we – our
> you – your   she – her   they – their
>
> *They're* students. *Their* teacher is Ms. Jones.
> *Mike* is a student. *His* sister is a student too.
>
> Singular nouns form the possessive by adding *'s.*
>
> This is *Joan's* desk.

C. Complete with the possessive adjective that refers to the subject of the first sentence.

EXAMPLE

Mike and Susan are students. ___*Their*___ books are on the desk.

1. Mike is a student. _____ sister is a student too.
2. Susan is a student. _____ brother is a student too.
3. I'm a lawyer. _____ pen is on the desk.
4. You're a teacher. _____ books are on the desk.
5. You and I are students. _____ notebooks are here.
6. Mike and Susan are students. _____ school is in the city.
7. Dick lives at home. _____ mother is a nurse.
8. We work in the city. _____ friends work in the city too.

Pronunciation and Intonation Practice

A. Repeat several times.

n as in *in*:	on, pen, man, ten, then, name, not, near, new
ng as in *long*:	morning, evening
m as in *map*:	am, many, much, room, me, my, time
v as in *have*:	of, five, leave, twelve, arrive, very
b as in *by*:	bus, book, boy, big, begin, before, both

B. Listen and repeat.

EXAMPLE

She's at work.   Is she at work?

1. He's at home.   Is he at home?
2. They're at their desks.   Are they at their desks?
3. She's a nurse.   Is she a nurse?
4. It's eleven o'clock.   Is it eleven o'clock?
5. We're at work.   Are you at work?

General Practice

A. Answer the questions.

EXAMPLE

What month did Tony move here from Houston?
He moved here from Houston in March.

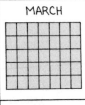

MARCH

1. What month did Tony get his job with the insurance company?

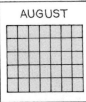

APRIL

2. What month did he meet Dick?

AUGUST

3. What month does school begin?

SEPTEMBER

4. What month did Joan move into her apartment?

FEBRUARY

5. What month did Tony move into his new apartment?

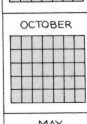

OCTOBER

6. What month does school end?

MAY

B. Conversation. Your teacher will ask you these questions or others like them. The questions will ask about things you can see or things you know about from your own experience. Give *real* answers to the questions.

What's your name?
What do you do?
What month is it?
What day of the week is it?
What time is it now?
Is that your book?
What color is your book?
Where is your book?
Is that your pen?
What color is your pen?
Where is your pen?

Reading and Oral Practice

A. Listen and repeat.

Where does Dick work?
He works in an office building downtown.

Is it an old or a new building?
It's an old building.

Does Dick like the building?
No, he doesn't like it at all.

What's the matter with the building?
There isn't any place to park.

Where does Dick park?
He parks in a garage.

Is the garage near the office?
No, it's three blocks away.

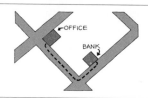

Are there any stores in the building?
Yes, there are a few stores on the ground floor.

Is there a bank nearby?
Yes, there's a bank around the corner.

Are there a lot of restaurants nearby?
No, there aren't many restaurants nearby.

Where does Dick eat lunch?
He eats lunch in a cafeteria.

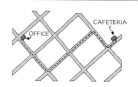

Is it near the office?
No, it's several blocks away.

Does Dick like to go to the cafeteria?
Yes, but he doesn't have much time for lunch.

> *At all* is frequently used with a negative to make it more emphatic.

B. Answer the questions.

1. Where does Dick work?

2. Is it an old or a new building?

3. Does Dick like the building?

4. What's the matter with the building?

5. Where does Dick park?

6. Is the garage near the office?

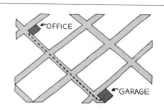

7. Are there any stores in the building?

8. Is there a bank nearby?

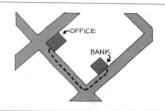

9. Are there a lot of restaurants nearby?

10. Where does Dick eat lunch?

11. Is it near the office?

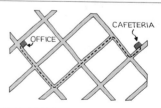

12. Does Dick like to go to the cafeteria?

10:00 A.M.   It's ten o'clock in the morning.

11:15 A.M.   It's eleven fifteen in the morning.

12:00 M.   It's noon.

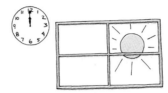

2:20 P.M.   It's two twenty in the afternoon.

3:25 P.M.   It's three twenty-five in the afternoon.

5:10 P.M.   It's five ten in the evening.

8:30 P.M.   It's eight thirty in the evening.

11:00 P.M.   It's eleven o'clock in the evening.
It's eleven o'clock at night.

12:00 P.M.   It's midnight.

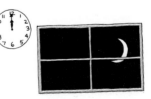

1:40 A.M.   It's one forty in the morning.
It's one forty at night.

4:15 A.M.   It's four fifteen in the morning.
It's four fifteen at night.

D. Answer the question "What time is it?"

1. 10:00 A.M.

2. 10:40 A.M.

3. 11:15 A.M.

4. 12:00 P.M.

5. 1:30 P.M.

6. 2:20 P.M.

7. 3:25 P.M.

8. 5:10 P.M.

9. 7:05 P.M.

10. 8:30 P.M.

11. 11:00 P.M.

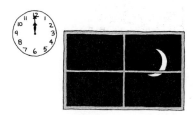

12. 12:00 A.M.

13. 1:40 A.M.

14. 4:15 A.M.

15. 6:20 A.M.

16. 8:55 A.M.

Diane Wu lives in the same apartment building as Joan Rossi and Tony Martinez.

TONY:	Good morning.
DIANE:	Oh, hi.
TONY:	My name's Tony Martinez. I just moved into apartment 4B.
DIANE:	Yes, I saw your car. I'm in 3A. My name's Diane Wu. You have a lot of laundry there.
TONY:	Well, when you move, you know. I need to get to a laundry.
DIANE:	There are a washer and dryer down in the basement.
TONY:	Oh, great! Say, is there a drugstore around here too?
DIANE:	Yes, right around the corner.
TONY:	I need to get a lot of things. What about a grocery?
DIANE:	There's a little store a block down the street.
TONY:	No supermarket?
DIANE:	No, there aren't any around here, but the little store has almost everything.
TONY:	Okay, thanks a lot.
DIANE:	You're welcome.

> *Just* is used with a past tense verb to indicate a very recent past action.
>
> *Say* can be used as an interjection, like *oh* or *well*.

Structure and Pattern Practice

There is (There's) and *There are* are used to introduce expressions with an unidentified noun and a phrase giving location or place. Instead of saying "A clock is on the wall," we say "There's a clock on the wall." *There's* is used before a singular noun and *There are* before a plural.

There's a bank around the corner.
There are some stores on the ground floor.

A. Complete with *There's* or *There are*.

EXAMPLE

_____There's_____ a bank around the corner.

1. _____ seven clerks in the office.
2. _____ a garage three blocks away.
3. _____ some cups in the kitchen.
4. _____ some bread on the table.
5. _____ a telephone on my desk.

In questions, *is* and *are* come before *there*.

Is there any mail this morning?
Are there any packages this morning?

B. Change to questions.

EXAMPLE

There's a cafeteria nearby.   *Is there a cafeteria nearby?*

1. There's a notebook in the top drawer.
2. There are a lot of stores on the ground floor.
3. There's a calendar on her desk.
4. There are three drawers in the desk.

Negatives are formed with *There is* and *There are* by placing *not* after *is* or *are*.

> There isn't any place to park.
> There aren't any restaurants in the building.

There are two classes of nouns in English, count nouns and mass nouns. Count nouns are those that can be counted: *one letter, two packages, three buildings*, etc. Mass nouns refer to things we do not usually count: *mail, paper, money, coffee*, etc.

Much is used only with mass nouns. *Many* is used only with plural count nouns. Both are usually used only in negative sentences after a verb.

> There isn't much mail this morning.
> There aren't many letters for Mr. Wilson.

C. Change to the negative. Use *much* or *many*.

EXAMPLE

There's a lot of mail this morning.   *There isn't much mail this morning.*

1. There's a lot of paper on Dick's desk.
2. There are a lot of books on the table.
3. There are a lot of stamps in the top drawer.
4. There are a lot of trucks in the garage.
5. There's a lot of water in the glass.
6. There's a lot of bread on the table.
7. There are a lot of pictures on the wall.
8. There are a lot of sentences on the chalkboard.
9. There's a lot of coffee in the kitchen.
10. There's a lot of money in the bottom drawer.

> *Some* and *any* are used with plural count nouns or mass nouns. After verbs, *some* is used in affirmative sentences and *any* is used in negative sentences.
>
> I have some coffee, but you don't have any coffee.
> She has some envelopes, but I don't have any envelopes.

D. Change to the affirmative.

EXAMPLE

There aren't any restaurants nearby.   *There are some restaurants nearby.*

1. There aren't any people in the restaurant.
2. There isn't any paper on my desk.
3. There aren't any magazines on the table.
4. There isn't any milk in the kitchen.
5. There isn't any coffee in the cup.
6. There aren't any pens and pencils in the top drawer.
7. There isn't any money in her purse.
8. There aren't any computers in the office.
9. There isn't any water on the floor.
10. There aren't any salesclerks in the store now.
11. There aren't any notebooks on the floor.
12. There aren't any students in the classroom.
13. There isn't any bread in the kitchen.
14. There aren't any trucks in the garage.
15. There isn't any money in his pocket.
16. There isn't any milk in the bottle.

Pronunciation and Intonation Practice

A. Repeat several times.

f as in *for*:   first, family, four, five, Friday, friend, from
v as in *have*:   leave, live, arrive, of, eleven, very, twelve
w as in *we*:   week, well, went, want, work
y as in *yes*:   yet, you, your, year, young
h as in *he*:   his, her, hello, have, house, home, who, how

B. Listen and repeat.

EXAMPLE

There's a book on the floor.

There's a book on the floor.

1. There's some *money* on the desk.
   There's some money on the *desk*.

2. There's some *water* on the table.
   There's some water on the *table*.

3. There's a *cup* on the desk.
   There's a cup on the *desk*.

4. There's a *pen* on the table.
   There's a pen on the *table*.

5. There's an *apple* in the kitchen.
   There's an apple in the *kitchen*.

General Practice

What month is it?
How many months are there in a year?
What day of the week is it?
How many days are there in a week?
How many students are there in the class?
Are many students absent today?
How many desks are there in the classroom?
How many windows are there in the classroom?
How many doors are there?
Are there any pictures on the wall?
How many books are there on your desk?
Are there any books on the floor?
Are there any notebooks on the floor?
Is there any paper on the floor?
Is there any money on your desk?

LESSON

3

THREE

Reading and Oral Practice

A. Listen and repeat.

Does Dick have a vacation every year?
Yes, he has two weeks off.

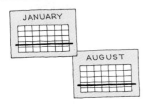

When does he take his vacation?
He takes one week in the winter and one week in the summer.

Why does he take a week in the winter?
Because he likes to go skiing.

Does he like any other winter sports?
Yes, he likes ice skating too.

Where does he go on his winter vacation?
He goes to a hotel in the mountains.

Does it snow in the mountains?
Yes, it snows a lot there.

Does Dick go to the mountains in the summer too?
No, he usually goes to the beach.

Why does he go to the beach?
He likes to go swimming.

What else does he like to do?
He likes to go sailing too.

Do his friends go to the beach too?
Yes, they like to go swimming too.

Do they stay in a hotel?
No, they drive back and forth every day.

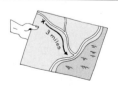

Do they live a long way from the beach?
No, they live near the beach. It's only a few minutes away.

B. Answer the questions.

1. Does Dick have a vacation every year?

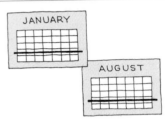

2. When does he take his vacation?

3. Why does he take a week in the winter?

4. Does he like any other winter sports?

5. Where does he go on his winter vacation?

6. Does it snow in the mountains?

7. Does Dick go to the mountains in the summer too?

8. Why does he go to the beach?

9. What else does he like to do?

10. Do his friends go to the beach too?

11. Do they stay in a hotel?

12. Do they live a long way from the beach?

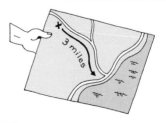

Where does Dick live?
He lives near New York.

Is it hot or cold in New York in the winter?
It's cold in the winter.

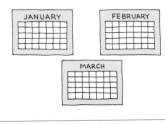

What months are very cold?
January, February, and March are usually cold.

When does spring begin?
It begins late in March.

Is the weather hot or cold in the spring?
It's usually warm in the spring.

What are the spring months?
April, May, and June are the spring months.

Is it hot or cold in the summer?
It's usually very hot in the summer.

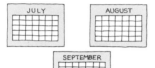

What months are very hot?
July, August, and September are usually hot.

When does fall begin?
It begins late in September.

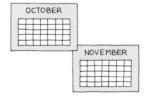

What's another name for fall?
Autumn is another name for fall.

Is the weather hot or cold in the fall?
It's usually cool in the fall.

What are the fall months?
October and November are the fall months.

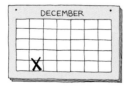

When does winter begin?
It begins late in December.

D. Answer the questions.

1. Where does Dick live?

2. Is it hot or cold in New York in the winter?

3. What months are very cold?

4. When does spring begin?

5. Is the weather hot or cold in the spring?

6. What are the spring months?

7. Is it hot or cold in the summer?

8. What months are very hot?

9. When does fall begin?

10. What's another name for fall?

11. Is the weather hot or cold in the fall?

12. What are the fall months?

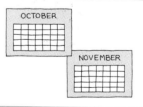

13. When does winter begin?

SALLY: When do you take your winter vacation?

DICK: I usually take it during the second or third week of January.

SALLY: Do you like to ski?

DICK: Yes, I love to go skiing.

SALLY: Where do you go?

DICK: To a hotel in the mountains.

SALLY: Is it far from here?

DICK: It's about a hundred miles away.

SALLY: Does it get cold?

DICK: Oh, yes, very cold!

SALLY: Do you go alone?

DICK: A couple of my friends usually go with me. Do you want to come along some weekend?

SALLY: No, not me. I don't like cold weather.

DICK: I really like it. I love snow!

A *mile* is an English measure of distance. A kilometer is five-eighths of a mile.

Note that *to get* can be followed by an adjective.

It gets hot in New York in the summer.

The expression *a couple of* followed by a noun refers to two things or people considered together.

Structure and Pattern Practice

> The simple present tense is used for an action that is habitual or customary or frequently repeated in the present. All verbs except *to be* use the simple or infinitive form, but in the third person singular, *s* or *es* is added to the base form.
>
> | | |
> |---|---|
> | I begin | we begin |
> | you begin | you begin |
> | he begins | |
> | she begins | they begin |
> | it begins | |
>
> The third person singular form of *to have* is *has*.
>
> She has a new car.

A. Change *I* to *she* in these sentences.

EXAMPLE

I work in an office.   *She works in an office.*

1. I go to the beach every summer.
2. I love to go skiing in February.
3. I like ice skating.
4. I stay at a hotel in the mountains.
5. I drive back and forth every day.

B. Change *he* to *they* in these sentences.

EXAMPLE

He works in an office.   *They work in an office.*

1. He has a small house.
2. He goes skiing every winter.
3. He begins work at nine o'clock in the morning.
4. He comes to work by subway.
5. He eats lunch at noon every day.

> Questions are formed by placing *do* or *does* before the subject. *Do* and *does* are always followed by the simple (infinitive) form of the verb.
>
> | | |
> |---|---|
> | Do I begin . . .? | Do we begin . . .? |
> | Do you begin . . .? | Do you begin . . .? |
> | Does he begin . . .? ⎫ | |
> | Does she begin . . .? ⎬ | Do they begin . . .? |
> | Does it begin . . .? ⎭ | |

C. Change to questions.

EXAMPLE

He works in an office.   *Does he work in an office?*

1. We see a lot of movies. (you)
2. She opens the office every morning.
3. He gets the mail early in the morning.
4. I park on the street. (you)
5. It snows a lot in the winter.
6. He reads a book every week.
7. She has a big house.
8. They take the subway to work.

> In questions with question words, the question word comes before *do* or *does*.
>
> When do we begin a new lesson?
> Where does he go in the winter?

D. Change to questions. Use the question words indicated.

EXAMPLE

They stay in a small hotel. (where)   *Where do they stay?*

1. I study accounting. (what) (you)
2. She gets up at seven o'clock. (what time)

3. He gets the mail in the morning. (when)
4. He eats lunch at a cafeteria. (where)
5. Fifteen students attend the class every day. (how many)
6. I see my family on the weekend. (when) (you)
7. He comes to work by car. (how)
8. He writes twenty letters every day. (how many)

Negatives are formed by placing *don't* or *doesn't* before the main verb. These contracted forms of *do not* and *does not* are generally used both in speech and in writing. They are always followed by the simple form of the main verb.

I don't begin . . .	We don't begin . . .
You don't begin . . .	You don't begin . . .
He doesn't begin . . .	
She doesn't begin . . . }	They don't begin . . .
It doesn't begin . . .	

E. Change to the negative.

EXAMPLE

He works in an office.   *He doesn't work in an office.*

1. She goes to the store every morning.
2. March follows January.
3. I have three sisters.
4. She does her homework in the morning.
5. We hurry to class every morning.
6. I like ice skating.
7. She writes letters for the manager.
8. The workday ends at three o'clock.
9. They study accounting.
10. He parks in a garage.

Pronunciation and Intonation Practice

A. Repeat several times.

k as in *clock*: like, talk, take, walk, look, come
g as in *big*: girl, begin, get, got, good
l as in *live*: leave, late, long, like, lawyer, last, alone
r as in *red*: rest, room, read, write, arrive, around

B. Listen and repeat.

EXAMPLE

It snows a lot.

1. He talks a lot.
2. He eats a lot.
3. She works a lot.
4. They ski a lot.
5. We study a lot.

C. Listen and repeat.

EXAMPLE

Do you like to study?

1. Do they have a small house?
2. Do they stay at a hotel?
3. Does she work here?
4. Does he drive to work?
5. Do you take a winter vacation?

D. Listen and repeat.

EXAMPLE

Where do you eat?

1. What does he read?
2. When does he leave?
3. When does the bus arrive?
4. What time does the class end?
5. What time does the store open?

General Practice

Conversation. Give *real* answers to these questions and to others like them that your teacher will ask.

Where do you live?
What time do you get up?
What time do you leave home?
How do you come to school?
Does school begin at _____ ?
Do you have English _____ days a week?
Do you eat lunch at _____ ?
Where do you eat lunch?
Does school end at _____ ?
What time do you usually get home?
Where do you eat dinner?
What do you usually do in the evening?
What kind of weather do you like?
What kind of sports do you like?
In what month does school usually begin?
In what month does school usually end?

LESSON

4

FOUR

Reading and Oral Practice

A. Listen and repeat.

What did Michael do last year?
He attended college last year.

Did he have his final exams in May?
No, he didn't have his final exams in May. He had his final exams the first week of June.

Where did he go after the exams?
He went home for the summer.

What did he do there?
He got a summer job in a gas station.

What did he do at work?
He pumped gas.

What else did he do?
He checked the oil.

What else did he do?
He cleaned windshields.

Did he do anything else?
He put air in the tires.

How much money did he make during the summer?
He made a few hundred dollars.

Did he spend his money?
No, he didn't spend his money. He put it in the bank.

What did he use it for?
He used it for his college tuition.

Three irregular verbs are introduced in this lesson: *to make*, past tense *made*; *to put*, past tense *put*; and *to spend*, past tense *spent*.

> He makes a little money every summer.
> He made a lot of money last summer.

> She always puts her money in the bank.
> She put some money in the bank last week.

> She usually spends the summer in the mountains.
> She spent a lot of money last summer.

Note especially that in English, one spends both time and money.

Gas is a short form for *gasoline*.
Exam is a short form for *examination*.

B. Answer the questions.

1. What did Michael do last year?

2. Did he have his final exams in May?

3. Where did he go after the exams?

4. What did he do there?

5. What did he do at work?

6. What else did he do?

7. What else did he do?

8. Did he do anything else?

9. How much money did he make during the summer?

10. Did he spend his money?

11. What did he use it for?

C. Listen and repeat.

SUNDAY

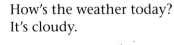

How's the weather today?
It's sunny today.

Is it hot or cold?
It isn't hot or cold; it's warm.

Is it a pleasant day?
It's a very pleasant day.

What season is it now?
It's spring.

MONDAY

How's the weather today?
It's cloudy.

Is it hot or cold?
It isn't hot or cold; it's cool.

Is it raining?
It's raining a little.

Is it a nice day?
No, it isn't a nice day at all.

TUESDAY

How's the weather today?
It's warm and sunny again.

Is it a nice day?
Yes, it's a very nice day.

Note that sentences about the weather have *it* as
the subject.

It's sunny today.
It's very warm too.
It's a pleasant day.

D. Answer the questions.

1. What day is it?
2. How's the weather today?
3. Is it hot or cold?
4. Is it a pleasant day?
5. What season is it now?

SUNDAY

6. What day is it?
7. How's the weather today?
8. Is it hot or cold?
9. Is it raining?
10. Is it a nice day?

MONDAY

11. What day is it?
12. How's the weather today?
13. Is it a nice day?

TUESDAY

E. Dialogue.

JOAN: How did you catch that cold?
DICK: I had a date last night.
JOAN: A date usually doesn't make you sick.
DICK: It did last night. You know my car?
JOAN: Yes, I know it. It's a wreck.
DICK: It didn't even get me to Vanessa's house last night.
JOAN: What happened?
DICK: I had a flat tire two blocks from my place.
JOAN: Well, it isn't too hard to change a tire.
DICK: But then it began to rain.
JOAN: Oh, that's right, it *did* rain last night.
DICK: It didn't just rain, it poured.
JOAN: So what did you do?
DICK: I just left the car and walked home.
JOAN: And what did Vanessa say about that?
DICK: Oh, she understands about my car.

To catch is an irregular verb. The past tense form is *caught*.

We catch a bus at this corner every morning.
She caught a cold last week.

To understand is also an irregular verb. The past tense form is *understood*.

She understands all about his car.
He understood the lesson yesterday.

Structure and Pattern Practice

The simple past tense is used for a completed action in the past. Regular verbs add *d* or *ed* to the simple form of the verb to form the past tense.

arrive   arriv*ed*   attend   attend*ed*

The same form is used for all persons.

I arrived	we arrived
you arrived	you arrived
he arrived	
she arrived	they arrived
it arrived	

A number of verbs already introduced have irregular past tense forms that must be memorized.

begin — began	go — went	say — said
catch — caught	have — had	see — saw
come — came	know — knew	spend — spent
do — did	leave — left	swim — swam
drive — drove	make — made	take — took
eat — ate	meet — met	understand — understood
get — got	put — put	write — wrote
give — gave	read — read	

A. Change to the past tense.

EXAMPLE

He attends college.   *He attended college.*

1. He puts the stamps on the desk.
2. We spend the summer at school.
3. I work during the summer.
4. The class begins at nine o'clock.
5. You make a little money during the summer.
6. She stays home on Wednesday.
7. They want to study accounting.
8. I take a bus to work.

Both questions and negatives are formed with the auxiliary verb *did*.

> *Did* he *arrive* on the third of May?
> He *didn't arrive* on the third of May.

The contracted form *didn't*, for *did not*, is commonly used both in speech and writing.

Did and *didn't* are always followed by the simple or infinitive form of the verb.

B. Change to questions.

EXAMPLE

He worked during the summer.   *Did he work during the summer?*

1. He took the packages to the store yesterday.
2. I studied programming last year. (you)
3. We copied the new sentences yesterday. (you)
4. He spent all his money.
5. She did all the homework last night.
6. They got back to school in September.
7. He put gas in a lot of cars last summer.
8. We had our final exams the last week of May. (you)

C. Change to questions. Use the question words indicated.

EXAMPLE

He worked at a filling station. (where)   *Where did he work?*

1. It rained a lot during April. (when)
2. They got to school at seven o'clock. (what time)
3. Twenty students attended the class. (how many)
4. She went to the mountains with her family. (where)
5. It snowed last Wednesday. (when)
6. I came to school by car. (how) (you)
7. We began a new lesson last Monday. (when) (you)
8. They ate lunch at a restaurant. (where)

I talked to the teacher.   *I didn't talk to the teacher.*

1. He used the money for his tuition.
2. We took a bus to the city.
3. She saw her family last summer.
4. He put air in the tires.
5. He checked the oil.
6. I got a flat tire.
7. They watched television last night.
8. He washed the windshield.

Pronunciation and Intonation Practice

A. Repeat several times.

a as in *day*:	late, they, take, name, mail, stay, eight, say
i as in *time*:	I'm, my, by, five, nine, drive, night, why
o as in *no*:	coat, go, home, so, alone, old, cold, open
a as in *all*:	wall, small, walk, talk, office, fall
ow as in *now*:	how, about, house, accounting, count
ou as in *you*:	new, school, who, two, do, noon, room
oo as in *book*:	good, look, put

B. Listen and repeat.

EXAMPLE

It rained yesterday.   It didn't rain today.

1. She walked to work yesterday.   She didn't walk to work today.
2. I worked last summer.   I didn't work this summer.
3. They rested yesterday.   They didn't rest today.
4. We studied yesterday.   We didn't study today.
5. He drove to work yesterday.   He didn't drive to work today.

General Practice

1. Is it cold in New York in January or in May?

2. Is January a summer month or a winter month?

3. Is it hot in New York in February or in August?

4. Is August a summer month or a winter month?

5. Is it warm in New York in April or in July?

6. Is April a spring month or a fall month?

7. Is it cool in New York in October or in January?

8. Is October a spring month or a fall month?

9. What's another name for fall?

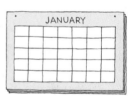

10. What's the first month of the year?

B. Conversation. Your teacher will ask you to perform actions like the ones below and then ask you questions to which you should give *real* answers.

Please put your book on _____ desk.
Did you put your book on _____ desk?
Please write your name on the chalkboard.
Did you write your name in your book?
Please walk to the door.
Did you walk to the window?
Please give your pencil to _____ .
Did you give your pencil to _____?
Please show _____ your notebook.
Did you show _____ your pencil?

5

F I V E

REVIEW

Structure and Pattern Practice

A. Change to the simple present tense.

EXAMPLE

He worked at a gas station.   *He works at a gas station.*

1. He used the money for his tuition.
2. She ate a big breakfast.
3. I parked in a garage.
4. They went to the beach.
5. The class began at nine o'clock.

B. Change to the simple past tense.

EXAMPLE

He makes a little money.   *He made a little money.*

1. She wants to go sailing.
2. He checks the oil.
3. We copy the sentences from the chalkboard.
4. I study computer programming.
5. You rest on Sunday.

C. Change *I* to *she* in these sentences.

EXAMPLE

I like to go swimming.   *She likes to go swimming.*

1. I spend the summer at the beach.
2. I put the money in the bank.
3. I take a bus to work.
4. I get up at six o'clock.
5. I clean the apartment on Saturday.

D. Change to questions.

E X A M P L E

He used the money for his tuition.   *Did he use the money for his tuition?*

1. She understood the lesson.
2. He's sick today.
3. They have a computer in the office.
4. She gave the package to the manager.
5. There's a bank near the office.
6. She has a computer at home.

E. Change to questions using the question word indicated in parentheses.

E X A M P L E

He worked at a gas station. (where)   *Where did he work?*

1. He worked at a gas station last summer. (when)
2. She put the stamps in the top drawer. (where)
3. I made a little money last summer. (how much) (you)
4. There are eleven students in the class. (how many)
5. She excused them at four o'clock. (what time)
6. There are a lot of magazines on the table. (how many)

F. Change to the negative.

E X A M P L E

He's in his office.   *He's not in his office.*

1. I park in a garage.
2. It's a new building.
3. She eats lunch at home.
4. He went to the bank.
5. We drive back and forth every weekend.
6. She takes her vacation in the winter.
7. She's on vacation this week.
8. I got a summer job.

G. Change to the negative. Remember to change *some* to *any* and *a lot of* to *much* or *many*, whichever is appropriate.

EXAMPLE

We eat a lot of bread.   *We don't eat much bread.*

1. There's a lot of mail this morning.
2. His assistant has some envelopes.
3. They used a lot of paper last week.
4. There are some stores on the ground floor.
5. We have a lot of time for lunch.
6. I saw some envelopes.
7. We have a lot of laundry to do.
8. They used a lot of stamps last month.
9. He spent a lot of money last summer.
10. She wrote a lot of sentences on the chalkboard.

General Practice

A. Answer the questions.

1. What's the last month of the year?

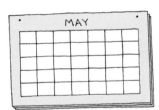

2. What month follows April?

3. What month comes after October?

4. Is it cloudy or sunny today?

B. Conversation. Give *real* answers to these questions and to others like them that your teacher will ask.

How many days a week do you have school?
Is today _____ ?
What time is it now?
How's the weather today?
Did it rain yesterday?
Did it snow yesterday?
Is this month _____ ?
How many students are there in the class?
Are many students absent today?
What time does school begin?
What time did you arrive at school today?
What time did you get up?
What time do you usually get up?
What time do you usually leave home?
What time did you leave home today?
Where did you eat dinner last night?
Where do you usually eat dinner?
What did you do yesterday evening?
What do you usually do in the evening?

Reading and Oral Practice

A. Listen and repeat.

What's Tony doing?
He's doing his chores.

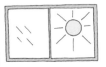

What time is it?
It's ten o'clock on Saturday morning.

Where is he now?
He's in the laundry room down in the basement.

What's he doing with his laundry?
He's taking it out of the washer and putting it
in the dryer.

What's Joan doing?
She's leaving the building.

Where is she going?
She's going downtown to shop.

What's she wearing?
She's wearing a coat.

What's she carrying?
She's carrying an umbrella.

What kind of day is it?
It's cold, and it looks like rain.

Where does Bill Morrissey live?
He lives in apartment 3D.

What does he like to do?
He likes to sleep late on Saturday.

What's he doing now?
He's just getting out of bed.

To wear and *to sleep* are irregular verbs. The past tense forms are *wore* and *slept*.

> She wore a coat yesterday.
> He slept late last Saturday.

In the expression *look like, like* is a preposition and is therefore followed by a noun.

> It looks *like a cold day.*

B. Answer the questions.

1. What's Tony doing?

---

2. What time is it?

---

3. Where is he now?

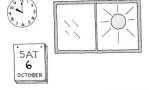

---

4. What's he doing with his laundry?

---

5. What's Joan doing?

6. Where is she going?

7. What's she wearing?

8. What's she carrying?

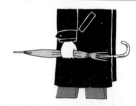

9. What kind of day is it?

10. Where does Bill Morrissey live?

11. What does he like to do?

12. What's he doing now?

C. Listen and repeat.

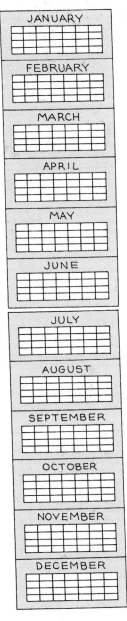

What's the first month of the year?
January is the first month of the year.

What's the second month?
February is the second month.

What's the third month?
March is the third month.

What's the fourth month?
April is the fourth month.

What's the fifth month?
May is the fifth month.

What's the sixth month?
June is the sixth month.

What's the seventh month?
July is the seventh month.

What's the eighth month?
August is the eighth month.

What's the ninth month?
September is the ninth month.

What's the tenth month?
October is the tenth month.

What's the eleventh month?
November is the eleventh month.

What's the twelfth month?
December is the twelfth month.

What's the last month of the year?
December is the last month of the year.

First, second, third, fourth, and so on, are known as ordinal numbers because they give the numerical order in which something occurs. Note that the first three are irregular. Note also the spelling of *eighth* and the change from *ve* to *f* in *five–fifth* and *twelve–twelfth.*

D. Answer the questions.

1. What's the first month of the year?

2. Is it usually hot or cold in January?

3. What's the second month?

4. What's the third month?

5. What's the fourth month?

6. What's the fifth month?

7. What's the sixth month?

8. What's the seventh month?

9. Is it usually hot or cold in July?

10. What's the eighth month?

11. What's the ninth month?

12. In what month does school usually begin?

13. What's the tenth month?

14. What's the eleventh month?

15. What's the twelfth month?

16. What's the last month of the year?

17. When does winter begin?

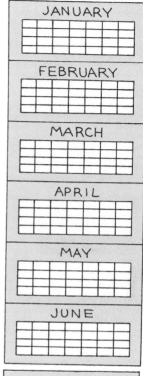

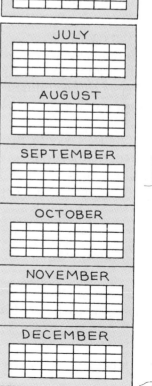

JANUARY

FEBRUARY

MARCH

APRIL

MAY

JUNE

JULY

AUGUST

SEPTEMBER

OCTOBER

NOVEMBER

DECEMBER

MIKE: Hey, look at that man! He's climbing that tree!

LINDA: It's all right, Mike, it's all right.

MIKE: What's going on? What are all these people doing here? Why is that guy climbing the tree?

LINDA: He's trying to get that ball out of the tree.

MIKE: What ball?

LINDA: Up there, see it?

MIKE: Oh, yeah. How did it get way up there?

LINDA: One of those children threw it.

MIKE: Hey, watch out! He's slipping!

LINDA: No, he's all right. He's just reaching for the ball.

MIKE: Look! He's waving his hand! He's got it!

LINDA: Well, thank goodness that's over.

MIKE: Where are you going now?

LINDA: Home. That really scared me.

Hey is an interjection used to try to get someone's attention.

Yeah is a common colloquial expression for *yes*.

Children is the irregular plural of the noun *child*.

Threw is the past tense form of the irregular verb *to throw*.

Over is used here in the sense of *finished*.

Structure and Pattern Practice

The present continuous, or present progressive, is used for an action that is going on now, at the present moment. The present continuous is formed with the present of *to be* and the present participle (the *-ing* form) of the verb.

I am hurrying.   You are hurrying.

The contracted forms are generally used in conversation.

I'm carrying   we're carrying
you're carrying   you're carrying
he's carrying
she's carrying }   they're carrying
it's carrying

The present participle is formed by adding *ing* to the basic form of the verb. If the verb ends in silent *e*, the *e* is dropped.

go—going   study—studying   live—living

A. Change to the present continuous. Change *every day* to *now*.

EXAMPLE

I drive to the city every day.   *I'm driving to the city now.*

1. She studies history every day.
2. He checks the mail every day.
3. The clerks come in every day.
4. She carries an umbrella every day.
5. I shop for groceries every day.
6. They have lunch at this restaurant every day.
7. He wears a coat every day.
8. We study the lesson every day.

B. Change to the simple present tense. Change *now* to *every day.*

EXAMPLE

I'm driving to the city now.　　*I drive to the city every day.*

1. We're having an English class now.
2. She's eating dinner at home now.
3. He's walking to school now.
4. He's taking the mail around to the offices now.
5. I'm doing my homework now.
6. I'm working in the office now.
7. She's studying accounting now.
8. They're watching television now.

Questions are formed by placing the form of *to be* before the subject.

Am I starting . . .?　　　Are we starting . . .?
Are you starting . . .?　　Are you starting . . . .?
Is he starting . . .?
Is she starting . . .?　　}　Are they starting . . .?
Is it starting . . .?

C. Change to questions.

EXAMPLE

I'm driving to the city now. (you)　　*Are you driving to the city now?*

1. They're staying home this evening.
2. He's wearing his coat today.
3. They're writing on the chalkboard now.
4. It's raining today.
5. He's walking to the bank now.
6. We're finishing our homework now. (you)
7. The typists are having lunch now.
8. She's putting stamps on the letters.

Pronunciation and Intonation Practice

A. Listen and repeat.

EXAMPLE

We're studying now.   We study every day.

1. I'm working now.   I work every day.
2. They're reading now.   They read every day.
3. He's writing now.   He writes every day.

B. Repeat several times.

i as in *pin*	*e* as in *pen*
bit	bet
tin	ten
till	tell
will	well
bid	bed

General Practice

Conversation. Your teacher will ask you some questions and will also ask you to perform actions like the ones below and then ask you questions about them. Give *real* answers to all the questions.

What book are we studying this year?
What book did we study last year?
What lesson are we studying this week?
What lesson did we study last week?
Walk around the room.
What are you doing? What did you do?
Write a sentence on the chalkboard.
What are you doing? What did you do?
Copy the sentence in your notebook.
What are you doing? What did you do?

Reading and Oral Practice

A. Listen and repeat.

Is Dick taking a bus to work?
No, he's driving to work.

What's he doing now?
He's listening to his car radio.

Why is he listening to his radio?
Because he wants to hear the traffic and weather
reports.

Is there a lot of traffic this morning?
There's a lot of traffic every morning.

What's Dick doing now?
He's stopping for a red light.

What's the police officer doing?
He's directing the traffic.

Is he motioning the drivers to wait?
No, he isn't motioning them to wait. He's motioning them to go ahead.

Why are the drivers blowing their horns?
Because they're in a hurry.

Why is the traffic so bad today?
Because it's raining.

What's Dick doing now?
He's looking for a place to park his car.

Is it easy to find a parking place?
No, it isn't easy to find a parking place. It's very difficult.

> *To hear, to blow,* and *to find* are irregular verbs.
>
> He hears the weather report every day.
> He heard the weather report yesterday.
>
> She blows the horn at every corner.
> She blew the horn at the last corner.
>
> I find a place to park every morning.
> I found a place to park yesterday morning.

B. Answer the questions.

1. Is Dick taking a bus to work?

2. What's he doing now?

3. Why is he listening to his radio?

4. Is there a lot of traffic this morning?

5. What's Dick doing now?

6. What's the police officer doing?

7. Is he motioning the drivers to wait?

8. Why are the drivers blowing their horns?

9. Why is the traffic so bad today?

10. What's Dick doing now?

11. Is it easy to find a parking place?

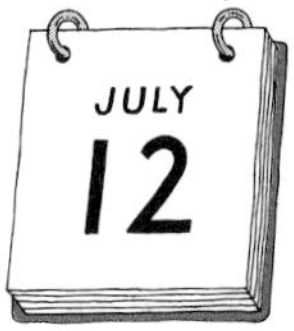

JULY 12

What's the date today?
It's the twelfth of July.

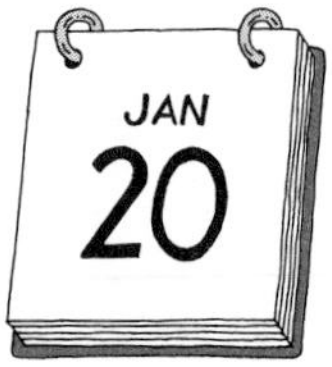

JAN 20

What's the date today?
It's the twentieth of January.

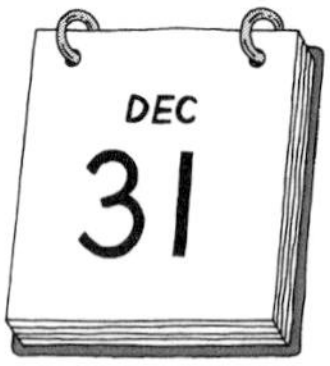

DEC 31

What's the date today?
It's the thirty-first of December.

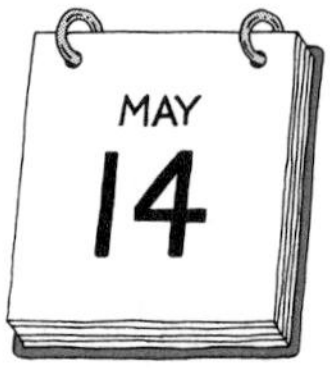

MAY 14

What's the date today?
It's the fourteenth of May.

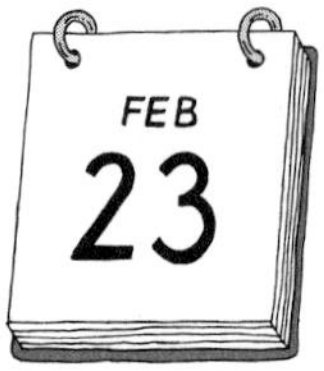

FEB 23

What's the date today?
It's the twenty-third of February.

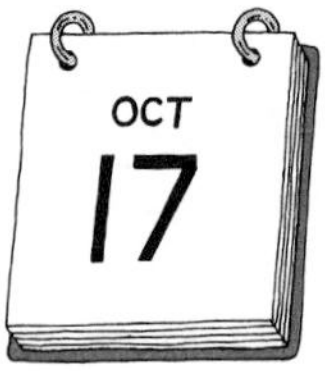

OCT 17

What's the date today?
It's the seventeenth of October.

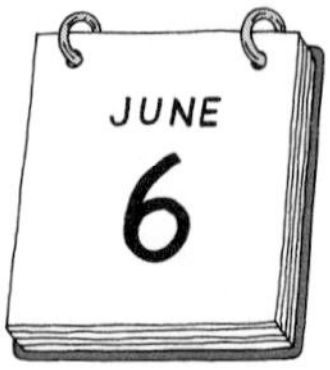

JUNE 6

What's the date today?
It's the sixth of June.

D. Answer the questions.

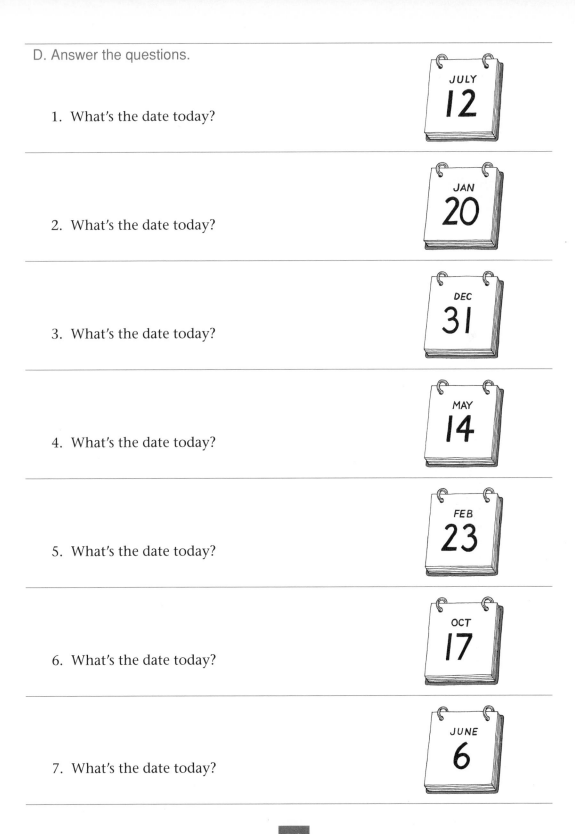

1. What's the date today?

JULY 12

2. What's the date today?

JAN 20

3. What's the date today?

DEC 31

4. What's the date today?

MAY 14

5. What's the date today?

FEB 23

6. What's the date today?

OCT 17

7. What's the date today?

JUNE 6

MAN: What are you doing?

DICK: I'm parking my car here.

MAN: No, I'm sorry, that isn't possible.

DICK: Why not? I don't see a "No Parking" sign.

MAN: This is my parking place.

DICK: I don't see a sign with your name.

MAN: I park here every day.

DICK: Well, I'm parking here today.

MAN: Why don't you look for another place?

DICK: Because there's a place here.

MAN: But it's my place!

DICK: Not today. I'm not moving my car.

MAN: There's a garage around the corner.

DICK: Good. *You* go and park there.

Sorry is the customary expression of regret.

Structure and Pattern Practice

The negative for the present continuous is formed by placing *not* after the form of *to be*.

I am not driving to work.
He is not going with us.
We are not waiting for him.

Note the contracted forms *isn't* and *aren't*. There is no contraction for *am not*.

I'm not waiting   we aren't waiting
you aren't waiting   you aren't waiting
he isn't waiting
she isn't waiting }   they aren't waiting
it isn't waiting

A. Change to the negative. Use the contracted forms *isn't* and *aren't* when possible.

EXAMPLE

He's looking for a parking place.   *He isn't looking for a parking place.*

1. The class is starting now.
2. He's attending college.
3. We're studying accounting.
4. I'm listening to the car radio.
5. They're watching television.
6. You're putting the books on the floor.
7. We're copying the new words in our notebooks.
8. She's talking to the professor.
9. I'm wearing a coat today.
10. The bus is stopping at the corner.

B. Change to the affirmative.

EXAMPLE

He isn't looking for a parking place.   *He's looking for a parking place.*

1. You aren't studying history.
2. They aren't putting their notebooks on the floor.
3. We aren't beginning Lesson 12 this week.
4. You aren't assigning a lot of homework.
5. We aren't copying the sentences in our books.
6. I'm not putting the stamp on the letter.
7. The drivers aren't blowing their horns.
8. He isn't taking the subway to work this week.
9. The bus isn't leaving.
10. We aren't looking for our notebooks.

Forms such as *you aren't* and *he isn't* can be used freely as alternatives to the forms *you're not, he's not,* etc., which were presented earlier.

we're not cold = we aren't cold
he's not working = he isn't working

C. Change to a different contracted form when possible.

EXAMPLE

He's not moving his car today.   *He isn't moving his car today.*

1. We're not studying Lesson 5 this week.
2. It's not raining today.
3. I'm not driving to the city today.
4. They're not stopping for the red light.
5. You're not parking in my place.
6. She's not writing the sentences in her notebook.
7. It's not cloudy today.
8. She's not a doctor.

Pronunciation and Intonation Practice

A. Listen and repeat.

EXAMPLE

He's taking the bus.   He isn't taking the train.

1. She's opening the letters.   She isn't opening the packages.
2. We're copying the sentences.   We aren't copying the new words.
3. They're moving the table.   They aren't moving the desk.

B. Repeat several times.

e as in *men*	*a* as in *man*
bet	bat
set	sat
bed	bad
pen	pan
beck	back

General Practice

Conversation. Your teacher will ask you to perform actions like the ones below and then ask you questions about them. Give *real* answers to the questions.

Walk around the desk.
Are you walking to the window?
Write a sentence on the chalkboard.
Are you writing in your notebook?
Copy the sentence in your notebook.
Are you copying the sentence in your book?
Look at page 70 in your book.
Are you looking at page 72?
Show _____ your pencil.
Are you showing _____ your book?

LESSON

8

EIGHT

Reading and Oral Practice

A. Listen and repeat.

What are we going to have soon?
We're going to have a long weekend soon.

What's Monday going to be?
It's going to be a holiday.

What kind of week did Joan have?
She had a very busy week.

What's she going to do over the weekend?
She's going to stay home and rest over the weekend.

What's Bill Morrissey going to do?
He's going to visit some friends.

Where do his friends live?
They live out in the country.

What does Bill like to do?
He likes to get out of the city.

What does he want to do in the country?
He wants to get some fresh air.

What's he going to do?
He's going to play tennis and go swimming.

What does Tony want to do?
He wants to stay in the city.

What's he going to do?
He's going to have fun every night.

How is he going to have fun?
He's going to make a date and go dancing every night.

B. Answer the questions.

1. What are we going to have soon?

2. What's Monday going to be?

3. What kind of week did Joan have?

4. What's she going to do over the weekend?

5. What's Bill Morrissey going to do?

6. Where do his friends live?

7. What does Bill like to do?

8. What does he want to do in the country?

9. What's he going to do?

10. What does Tony want to do?

11. What's he going to do?

12. How is he going to have fun?

C. Listen and repeat.

What's the date today?
The date today is June sixteenth.
What's the date going to be tomorrow?
The date tomorrow is going to be June seventeenth.

Is today August thirtieth?
No, today isn't August thirtieth. It's August thirty-first.

Is today May thirteenth?
No, today isn't May thirteenth. It's May twelfth.

Is there a holiday this month?
Yes, there's a holiday on September third.

Is there a holiday this month?
Yes, there's a holiday on October twelfth.

Is there a holiday this month?
There are two holidays this month. There's a holiday on November eleventh. There's another holiday on November twenty-eighth.

D. Answer the questions.

1. What's the date today?

2. What's the date going to be tomorrow?

3. Is today August thirtieth?

4. Is today May thirteenth?

5. Is there a holiday this month?

6. Is there a holiday this month?

7. Is there a holiday this month?

TONY: There's going to be a holiday on Monday.

JOAN: Yes, I know.

TONY: Do you have any plans?

JOAN: Not really. I had a busy week. I'm just going to stay home and rest.

TONY: That doesn't sound like much fun.

JOAN: What are you going to do?

TONY: I'm going to a party Friday and dance all night.

JOAN: Then are you going to sleep all day Saturday?

TONY: Not me! I'm going to play ball Saturday morning.

JOAN: And Saturday night?

TONY: I'm going to try out that new disco downtown.

JOAN: And Sunday? And Monday?

TONY: I'm going to be busy every day. Every night too.

JOAN: It certainly sounds like fun — too much fun maybe.

Structure and Pattern Practice

> One way of expressing the future in English is with the phrase *to be going to* followed by the basic form of the verb.
>
> We're going to begin a new lesson tomorrow.
>
> The word *going* in such sentences does not indicate movement or motion but simply indicates future time.

A. Change to the *going to* future. Change *every day* to *tomorrow*.

EXAMPLE

She leaves early every day.   *She's going to leave early tomorrow.*

1. He visits his friends every day.
2. I write a lot of letters every day.
3. They rest every day.
4. He hurries to work every day.
5. We attend school every day.
6. The class begins at nine o'clock every day.
7. She takes a bus to the city every day.
8. They study English every day.

B. Change to the *going to* future. Change *now* to *tomorrow*.

EXAMPLE

She's studying English now.   *She's going to study English tomorrow.*

1. It's raining now.
2. They're starting a new lesson now.
3. He's looking for a job now.
4. I'm copying the sentences in my notebook now.
5. He's meeting his friends now.
6. She's playing tennis now.
7. We're putting air in the tires now.
8. You're writing a letter now.

Questions are formed by placing the form of *to be* before the subject.

Is he going to stay home this weekend?
Are they going to have an exam on Monday?

C. Change to questions.

EXAMPLE

He's going to stay home this weekend.   *Is he going to stay home this weekend?*

1. We're going to listen to the radio. (you)
2. She's going to stop at the corner.
3. I'm going to drive to the city tomorrow. (you)
4. It's going to be cold tomorrow.
5. She's going to walk to the bank.
6. I'm going to park my car here. (you)
7. They're going to have fun over the weekend.

Negatives are formed by placing *not* after the form of *to be*.

They're not going to watch television.
He isn't going to visit his friends this weekend.

D. Change to the negative. Use the contracted forms *isn't* and *aren't* when possible.

EXAMPLE

She's going to stop at the bank.   *She isn't going to stop at the bank.*

1. You're going to find a parking place near the office.
2. She's going to open the package.
3. I'm going to talk to the professor tomorrow.
4. We're going to take chemistry next year.
5. I'm going to move my car.
6. We're going to listen to the weather report.
7. There's going to be a holiday next week.

Pronunciation and Intonation Practice

A. Listen and repeat.

EXAMPLE

They're going to work tomorrow.

1. It's going to rain tomorrow.
2. We're going to study tomorrow.
3. She's going to rest tomorrow.
4. He's going to sleep tomorrow.
5. They're going to ski tomorrow.

B. Repeat several times.

i as in *bit*	*e* as in *bet*	*a* as in *bat*
sit	set	sat
bid	bed	bad
hid	head	had
tin	ten	tan
fin	fen	fan

General Practice

Conversation. Give *real* answers to these questions and to others like
them that your teacher will ask.

What time are you going to leave school today?
Where are you going after school?
How are you going to go home?
Where are you going to have dinner?
What are you going to do this evening?
What time are you going to get up tomorrow?
What time is school going to begin tomorrow?
What are you going to study tomorrow?
What time are you going to have lunch?
What are you going to eat for lunch?
When are you going to have a vacation?
What's the date today?
What's the date going to be tomorrow?

Reading and Oral Practice

A. Listen and repeat.

What evening was it?
It was Friday evening.

Why did Tony look in the refrigerator for something to eat?
Because he was very hungry.

What was there in the refrigerator?
There was a loaf of bread, but it was stale.

What was there to drink?
There wasn't anything to drink.

What did Tony decide to do?
He decided to go to the little store down the street.

What time was it when he got there?
It was after nine o'clock when he got there.

How was the store?
It was still crowded.

How were the shelves?
They were almost empty.

What do a lot of men and women do on Friday evening?
They do their shopping for the week on Friday evening.

Where did Tony finally decide to eat?
He finally decided to eat at the fast food place next door.

What did he have?
He had a hamburger, French fries, and a soft drink.

Was it a healthy meal?
No, it wasn't healthy at all.

English uses a form of *to be* and an adjective to express the ideas of hunger and thirst.

> I was very hungry. I needed something to eat.
> I was thirsty too. I wanted a drink.

To drink is an irregular verb. The past tense form is *drank*.

> That child drinks a lot of milk.
> She drank up all the milk in the house yesterday.

Men and *women* are the irregular plurals for *man* and *woman*.

B. Answer the questions.

1. What evening was it?

2. Why did Tony look in the refrigerator for something to eat?

3. What was there in the refrigerator?

4. What was there to drink?

5. What did Tony decide to do?

6. What time was it when he got there?

7. How was the store?

8. How were the shelves?

9. What do a lot of men and women do on Friday evening?

10. Where did Tony finally decide to eat?

11. What did he have?

12. Was it a healthy meal?

C. Listen and repeat.

BORN:
MARCH 7,
1970

How old is he?
He's twenty years old.
When was he born?
He was born in 1970.
When is his birthday?
His birthday is March seventh.

BORN:
JULY 23,
1974

How old is she?
She's sixteen years old.
When was she born?
She was born in 1974.
When is her birthday?
Her birthday is July twenty-third.

BORN:
APRIL 12,
1958

How old is this woman?
She's thirty-two years old.
When was she born?
She was born in 1958.
When is her birthday?
Her birthday is April twelfth.

BORN:
SEPTEMBER 29,
1945

How old is this man?
He's forty-five years old.
When was he born?
He was born in 1945.
When is his birthday?
His birthday is September twenty-ninth.

Note the verb *to be born. Was* or *were* is usually
used before *born.*

I was born in 1968.
They were born in 1970.

D. Answer the questions

1. How old is he?
   When was he born?
   When is his birthday?

BORN:
MARCH 7,
1970

2. How old is she?
   When was she born?
   When is her birthday?

BORN:
JULY 23,
1974

3. How old is this woman?
   When was she born?
   When is her birthday?

BORN:
APRIL 12,
1958

4. How old is this man?
   When was he born?
   When is his birthday?

BORN:
SEPTEMBER 29,
1945

5. How old are you?
   When were you born?
   When is your birthday?

Donna is a student in Dick's computer programming class.

DONNA:	Good evening, Dick.
DICK:	Hello, Donna. How was the lecture last night?
DONNA:	It was important. Interesting too. Where were you?
DICK:	I stayed home. I was very tired. I was a little sick.
DONNA:	What was the matter?
DICK:	I had a cold, I guess. I coughed and I sneezed all night.
DONNA:	That's too bad, but you sound all right today.
DICK:	I took a little cough medicine and a few vitamin pills and went to bed.
DONNA:	A lot of people have colds at this time of year.
DICK:	Did anybody else miss the lecture?
DONNA:	Yes, a few other students were absent.
DICK:	Did you take any notes?
DONNA:	Yes, I did.
DICK:	Oh, good! Please show them to me before class.

Structure and Pattern Practice

> *Was* and *were* are the past tense forms of *to be*.
>
> | I was | we were |
> |-------|---------|
> | you were | you were |
> | he was | |
> | she was | they were |
> | it was | |

A. Change to the past tense.

EXAMPLE

I am very tired.   *I was very tired.*

1. Three of the typists are absent.
2. There's a lot of mail today.
3. There are a lot of packages on the floor.
4. You're late this morning.
5. She's very busy today.
6. It's cold and cloudy this morning.

> Negatives are formed with *was not* (*wasn't*) and *were not* (*weren't*). The contractions are almost always used in both conversation and writing. Questions are formed by putting *was* or *were* before the subject.
>
> I wasn't absent yesterday.   Were the lectures interesting?

B. Change to questions.

EXAMPLE

He was very tired.   *Was he very tired?*

1. The bus was late.
2. The lecture was very important.
3. Mary was sick yesterday.
4. There were a lot of letters for the manager.
5. That book was interesting.
6. He was born in 1972.

Was and *were* are also used in sentences beginning with *there.*

Was there a lot of mail?
Yes, there was a lot of mail.

Were there a lot of letters?
Yes, there were a lot of letters.

Remember that *much* is used with mass nouns and *many* is used with plural count nouns. They are not commonly used after verbs in affirmative sentences.

There was a lot of homework last night.
There wasn't much homework last night.

There were a lot of students in the classroom.
There weren't many students in the classroom.

Remember also that *some* is used after verbs in affirmative sentences and *any* is used in negative sentences.

I took some cough medicine.
I didn't take any cough medicine.

C. Change to the negative. Use *much, many,* or *any* when appropriate.

EXAMPLE

There were some books on the floor.   *There weren't any books on the floor.*

1. There were a lot of people in the cafeteria.
2. There was a lot of paper in the desk.
3. There was some coffee in the cup.
4. There were some new clerks in the office.
5. There were some places to park near the office.
6. There was a lot of traffic this morning.
7. There were a lot of keys on the table.
8. There were a lot of cars on the street.
9. There was a lot of mail yesterday.
10. There was some water on the floor.

> *A little* is used with mass nouns and also with adjectives. *A few* is used with plural count nouns.
>
> There was *a little paper* on the desk.
> She was *a little sick* yesterday.
> There were *a few stamps* in the top drawer.

D. Complete these sentences with *a little* or *a few*, whichever is appropriate.

EXAMPLE

There was ___*a little*___ paper in the top drawer.

1. There were _____ envelopes in the desk.
2. There were _____ students absent last night.
3. There was _____ oil in the car.
4. There were _____ coats on the chair.
5. There was _____ coffee in the cup.
6. There was _____ bread on the table.

> *Anybody* and *nobody* are impersonal or indefinite pronouns. *Nobody* is a negative. Note that *not* does not occur in the same sentences as *nobody*.
>
> Did anybody help him?
> Nobody helped him.

E. Answer these questions with *nobody*.

EXAMPLE

Did anybody help Dick?   *Nobody helped Dick.*

1. Did anybody watch television last night?
2. Did anybody walk to work?
3. Did anybody get to work early?
4. Did anybody see that new movie?
5. Did anybody get sick this week?

Pronunciation and Intonation Practice

> Some of the negative contractions are pronounced as one syllable and some are pronounced as two syllables.

A. Repeat several times.

One syllable	*Two syllables*
aren't	is - n't
weren't	was - n't
don't	does - n't
	did - n't

B. Listen and repeat.

EXAMPLE

He was very tired.

1. The room was very small.
2. The lecture was very important.
3. We were very busy.
4. She was very thirsty.
5. The lesson was very difficult.

C. Repeat several times.

a as in *hat*	*o* as in *hot*
cat	cot
had	hod
mad	mod
tap	top
cap	cop
lack	lock
rack	rock
black	block

General Practice

Conversation. Give *real* answers to these questions and to others like them that your teacher will ask.

What day is today?
What day was yesterday?
What's tomorrow going to be?
How's the weather today?
How was the weather yesterday?
What month is this?
How many days are there in this month?
What was last month?
How many days were there last month?
What month were you born?
How many students are there in the class today?
How many were there in the class yesterday?
Were you absent yesterday?
Were you on time this morning?
Was there much homework last night?
Was there much traffic this morning?

LESSON

10
TEN

REVIEW

Structure and Pattern Practice

A. Change to the present continuous. Change *every day* to *now*.

EXAMPLE

We study every day.   *We're studying now.*

1. She listens to the radio every day.
2. He waits for his friends every day.
3. I park in a garage every day.
4. She writes a letter every day.
5. He takes the bus downtown every day.
6. They talk to their professor every day.
7. I walk to work every day.
8. It rains every day.

B. Change to the *going to* future. Change *every day* to *tomorrow*.

EXAMPLE

We study every day.   *We're going to study tomorrow.*

1. They wear their coats every day.
2. She rests every day.
3. I visit my friends every day.
4. They copy the sentences every day.
5. She opens the office every day.
6. He stays at home every day.
7. He assigns a lot of homework every day.
8. We watch television every day.

C. Change first to the present continuous and then to the *going to* future. Make the appropriate changes in the time words.

EXAMPLE

He studied yesterday.   *He's studying now.*
                          He's going to study tomorrow.

1. They wrote some letters yesterday.
2. The police officer directed traffic yesterday.
3. He looked for his book yesterday.
4. She ate breakfast yesterday.
5. I hurried to school yesterday.
6. We had a lot of fun yesterday.

D. Change to questions.

EXAMPLE

He's studying history now.   *Is he studying history now?*

1. The class is starting now.
2. I'm going to take the subway to work. (you)
3. They're looking for some stamps.
4. We're going to begin a new lesson tomorrow. (you)
5. She's talking to the manager now.
6. The bus is going to leave at nine o'clock tomorrow.

E. Change to the negative. Use both contracted forms when possible.

EXAMPLE

He's studying chemistry.   *He's not studying chemistry.*
                             He isn't studying chemistry.

1. She's looking for paper and envelopes.
2. The clerks are coming in now.
3. He's waiting for the bus now.
4. I'm checking the oil now.
5. They're going to live in the city.
6. They're cleaning the apartment today.

F. Change to the past. Change *today* to *yesterday.*

EXAMPLE

She's sick today.   *She was sick yesterday.*

1. We're very busy today.
2. It's very cold today.
3. She's very late today.
4. There's a lot of homework today.
5. There are a lot of students in the classroom today.
6. The lecture is very interesting today.
7. Two of the clerks are absent today.
8. The lesson is very difficult today.

G. Change to the negative. Use *much, many,* or *any* when appropriate.

EXAMPLE

She found some stamps.   *She didn't find any stamps.*

1. We had a lot of time to finish the exam.
2. There was a lot of oil in the car.
3. I see a lot of movies.
4. They watch a lot of television.
5. We ate some apples.
6. There are a lot of typists in the office.
7. There were some magazines on the table.
8. She gets a lot of letters.
9. He used some paper and some envelopes.
10. There were a lot of books on the desk.

H. Complete with *a little* or *a few,* whichever is appropriate.

EXAMPLE

There was ____*a little*____ paper in the top drawer.

1. We copied _____ sentences in our notebooks.
2. There was _____ money on the desk.
3. He carried _____ books to school.
4. We need _____ gas.
5. She put _____ bread on the table.
6. He took _____ vitamin pills last night.

General Practice

A. Answer the questions.

1. What's the first month of the year?
2. What's the second day of the week?
3. What's the third month of the year?
4. What's the fourth day of the week?
5. What's the fifth month of the year?
6. What's the sixth day of the week?
7. What's the seventh day of the week?
8. How many days are there in a week?
9. What's the eighth month of the year?
10. What's the ninth month of the year?
11. What's the tenth month of the year?
12. What's the eleventh month of the year?
13. What's the twelfth month of the year?
14. What's the last day of March?
15. How many months are there in a year?

JANUARY	FEBRUARY
MARCH	APRIL
MAY	JUNE
JULY	AUGUST
SEPTEMBER	OCTOBER
NOVEMBER	DECEMBER

MARCH

SUN	MON	TUES	WED	THURS	FRI	SAT
1	2	3	4	5	6	7
8	9	10	11	12	13	14
15	16	17	18	19	20	21
22	23	24	25	26	27	28
29	30	31				

B. Conversation. Give *real* answers to these questions and to others like them that your teacher will ask.

What lesson are you studying this week?
What lesson did you study last week?
What lesson are you going to study next week?
What time did your class begin today?
What time is it going to end?
How's the weather today? How was it yesterday?
Is school going to end in _____ ?
Is next month going to be _____ ?
How many students are there in class today?
How many students were there in class yesterday?
What month were you born?
When is your birthday?

ELEVEN

Reading and Oral Practice

A. Listen and repeat.

What did Diane buy?
She bought a new bed and dresser.

What does she want?
She wants the store to deliver them.

What did they tell her?
They'll deliver them only on Tuesday or Thursday morning.

Will they deliver them in the evening?
No, they won't deliver them in the evening.

Will they deliver them on the weekend?
No, they won't deliver them on the weekend.

Where will Diane be on Tuesday and Thursday morning?
She'll be at work on Tuesday and Thursday morning.

Why can't she be home?
She can't take a day off.

What did she finally do?
She asked Nancy Meyer to help her.

Where does Nancy live?
She lives in the apartment next door to Diane.

Why is Nancy home during the day?
Nancy is home during the day because she works at night.

What will she do for Diane?
She'll accept the furniture for Diane.

What else will she do?
She'll also sign the receipt for it.

> *To buy* and *to tell* are irregular verbs.
>
> I buy all my food at that store.
> He bought groceries Friday evening.
>
> I'll tell her to call you tomorrow.
> I told them to deliver the furniture on Friday.

B. Answer the questions.

1. What did Diane buy?

2. What does she want?

3. What did they tell her?

4. Will they deliver them in the evening?

5. Will they deliver them on the weekend?

6. Where will Diane be on Tuesday and Thursday morning?

7. Why can't she be home?

8. What did she finally do?

9. Where does Nancy live?

10. Why is Nancy home during the day?

11. What will she do for Diane?

12. What else will she do?

C. Listen and repeat.

What happened in 1492 [fourteen ninety-two]?
Columbus discovered America in 1492.

What happened in 1500 [fifteen hundred]?
Cabral discovered Brazil in 1500.

What happened in 1828 [eighteen twenty-eight]?
Webster published his dictionary in 1828.

What happened in 1867 [eighteen sixty-seven]?
Russia sold Alaska to the United States in 1867.

What happened in 1879 [eighteen seventy-nine]?
Edison invented the electric light bulb in 1879.

What happened in 1903 [nineteen oh three]?
The Wright brothers flew the first airplane in 1903.

Sold is the past tense form of the irregular verb *to sell*.

That store sells furniture.
They sold Diane a new bed and dresser last week.

Flew is the past tense form of the irregular verb *to fly*.

She flies a lot on business.
She flew to New York last month.

D. Answer the questions.

1. What happened in 1492?

COLUMBUS

2. What happened in 1500?

CABRAL

3. What happened in 1828?

WEBSTER

AMERICAN DICTIONARY

4. What happened in 1867?

1867 ALASKA

Russia → United States

5. What happened in 1879?

EDISON

6. What happened in 1903?

WRIGHT

E. Dialogue.

JOAN: You look happy.

TONY: I am, I am. My parents are coming for a visit.

JOAN: Oh, that's nice. When will they be here?

TONY: They'll get here on Wednesday.

JOAN: Are they driving?

TONY: No, they'll fly. It's a long trip by car, two or three days.

JOAN: Are they going to stay here with you?

TONY: No, this place isn't big enough. They'll stay at a hotel.

JOAN: How long will they be here?

TONY: For a week.

JOAN: What are you planning to do?

TONY: I'll take them sightseeing. There are a lot of things to see here. And I'll get some theater tickets.

JOAN: Don't forget to take them to some good restaurants.

TONY: I won't, I won't. We're going to have a really good time.

Parents includes one's father and one's mother.

The verb *to forget* is irregular.

He forgets to call his parents.
She forgot to do her homework last night.

Structure and Pattern Practice

> The future can be expressed by means of the auxiliary verb *will* followed by the simple form of the main verb.
>
> | | |
> |---|---|
> | I'll begin | we'll begin |
> | you'll begin | you'll begin |
> | he'll begin | |
> | she'll begin } | they'll begin |
> | it will begin | |
>
> The contracted forms are generally used in both speaking and informal writing.

A. Change to the future with *will*. Change *last* to *next*.

EXAMPLE

He worked in an office last summer.   *He'll work in an office next summer.*

1. They studied a lot last year.
2. She tried to see her professor last week.
3. I visited my family last month.
4. He looked for a job last week.
5. We began a new lesson last Monday.

> Questions are formed by placing *will* before the subject.
>
> Will they stay in a hotel?

B. Change to questions.

EXAMPLE

She'll start work on Monday.   *Will she start work on Monday?*

1. She'll study chemistry next year.
2. I'll see the manager on Tuesday. (you)
3. I'll put air in the tires on Wednesday. (you)
4. It will rain on Thursday.
5. We'll have an exam on Friday. (you)

Negatives are formed with the contracted form
won't (*will not*) followed by the main verb.

He won't return on Friday night.

C. Change to the negative.

EXAMPLE

He'll visit New York on this trip.   *He won't visit New York on this trip.*

1. They'll write the new words on the chalkboard.
2. She'll stay at the office after six o'clock.
3. I'll leave for Chicago on Monday morning.
4. They'll be in the office on Saturday.
5. We'll miss the lecture.
6. You'll forget the new words.

How long? is used to ask questions about the
duration of an action.

How long did he work at the gas station?
He worked there for eight weeks.

D. Change to questions with *How long?*

EXAMPLE

He'll stay at the hotel for three days.   *How long will he stay at the hotel?*

1. It's going to rain for two or three days.
2. I'm going to sleep for four hours. (you)
3. They're going to wait for a few minutes.
4. He studied accounting for eight months.
5. He'll be at the lecture all morning.
6. She'll study chemistry for a year.

Pronunciation and Intonation Practice

A. Listen and repeat.

EXAMPLE

I'll need six shirts.

1. They'll have three exams next month.
2. I'll wait five minutes.
3. I'll stay two nights.
4. We'll study four lessons this month.
5. We'll use three books this year.

B. Repeat several times.

i as in *it*	*ea* as in *eat*
sit	seat
lip	leap
hid	heed
tin	teen
wick	week
slip	sleep

General Practice

Conversation. Give *real* answers to these questions and to others like them that your teacher will ask.

What time did school begin today?
What time will it begin tomorrow?
What time will it end today?
What time will it end tomorrow?
Will you have an English class on Saturday?
Will you have an English class on Sunday?
When did we have our last holiday?
Will we have another holiday on _____ ?
When will we have our next holiday?
When will school end for the year?
How long a vacation will you have?
What are you going to do during the vacation?
When will school begin after the vacation?

LESSON
12
TWELVE

Reading and Oral Practice

A. Listen and repeat.

Is Dick going to stay at work all day?
No, he may go home early.

What's the matter with him?
He doesn't feel well today.

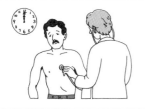

Is he going to see a doctor?
Yes, he can see his doctor at noon.

What will the doctor tell him?
The doctor may send him home.

What should Dick do at the office today?
He should take an inventory of the office supplies.

What must he do to take the inventory?
He must count everything in the supply room.

When must he finish the inventory?
He must finish it on Friday.

What should he do after the inventory?
He should order new supplies.

Does Dick like to take inventory?
No, he doesn't like to take inventory at all.

Why doesn't he like to do it?
Because he gets hot and dirty and sleepy.

Should he be careful with the inventory?
Yes, he should be very careful.

Can he get anyone else to help him?
No, he can't.

> *To feel* and *to send* are irregular verbs.
>
> She felt very tired last night.
> The doctor sent Dick home early.

B. Answer the questions.

1. Is Dick going to stay at work all day?

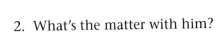

2. What's the matter with him?

3. Is he going to see a doctor?

4. What will the doctor tell him?

5. What should Dick do at the office today?

6. What must he do to take the inventory?

7. When must he finish the inventory?

8. What should he do after the inventory?

9. Does Dick like to take inventory?

10. Why doesn't he like to do it?

11. Should he be careful with the inventory?

12. Can he get anyone else to help him?

C. Listen and repeat.

What's the speed limit here?
It's twenty-five miles per hour.
How many kilometers is that?
It's forty kilometers per hour.

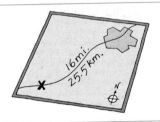

What's the distance from here to the city?
It's sixteen miles from here to the city.
How many kilometers is that?
It's about twenty-five and a half kilometers.

How far is it to the airport?
It's ten miles to the airport.
How many kilometers is that?
It's sixteen kilometers.

D. Answer the questions.

1. What's the speed limit here?
   How many kilometers is that?

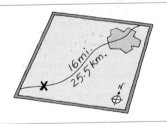

2. What's the distance from here to the city?
   How many kilometers is that?

3. How far is it to the airport?
   How many kilometers is that?

E. Dialogue.

BILL: You look angry. What's the matter?

DIANE: I just brought this blow dryer home this evening, and it doesn't work.

BILL: Where did you buy it?

DIANE: At that hardware store down the street.

BILL: You should take it back. You can exchange it for another one.

DIANE: No, I can't.

BILL: You must. You can't let them sell you a piece of junk.

DIANE: I know, I know, but I'm going to be out of town. I'm leaving early tomorrow morning.

BILL: Well, when are you coming back?

DIANE: Not for a month. It may even be six weeks.

BILL: You shouldn't just throw your money away. Is the store open now?

DIANE: No, it's too late. It closes at nine, and it's after that now. But maybe you can help me.

BILL: Do you want me to exchange it for you?

DIANE: Can you?

BILL: Well, I can do it on Saturday, I guess. But I'll need a receipt.

DIANE: Oh, Bill, thanks a lot! I have the receipt right here.

Brought is the past tense form of the irregular verb *to bring*. *To let* is also an irregular verb. The present and past tense forms are the same.

One is used here as a pronoun to take the place of a noun that has just been mentioned, in this case the *blow dryer*.

Structure and Pattern Practice

Many verb phrases in English are made up of the modal auxiliary verbs *can, may, should,* or *must* followed by the main verb. Like *will,* these auxiliary verbs do not change form and they are always followed by the simple form of the main verb. The modal auxiliaries can have either present or future significance, depending on the situation in which they are used.

I can begin	we can begin
you can begin	you can begin
he can begin	
she can begin	they can begin
it can begin	

Each modal auxiliary verb has a special area of meaning. *Can* indicates the physical or mental ability to perform an action.

He can finish the inventory in one day.
She can rest on Sunday.

A. Change these sentences so that they use verb phrases with *can*.

EXAMPLE

She walked to work.   *She can walk to work.*

1. We used the money for our tuition.
2. He rests on Saturday and Sunday.
3. He finished the inventory in a day.
4. They began a new lesson.

May indicates that the action is possible but not certain.

He may go home early (but he may not).

May is also used to ask for permission and to give it.

May I write in my book?
No, you may not write in your book. You may write in your notebook.

B. Change these sentences so that they use verb phrases with *may*.

EXAMPLE

He went home early.　　*He may go home early.*

1. He assigns a lot of homework.
2. He saw the doctor at noon.
3. She attended the lecture.
4. She slept a little on Sunday.

Should indicates an action which is advisable, or which the subject has a duty or obligation to perform.

He should be careful.　　She should study every night.

C. Change these sentences so that they use verb phrases with *should*.

EXAMPLE

They wore their coats.　　*They should wear their coats.*

1. He cleaned his apartment.
2. She checked the gas and oil.
3. We carried our umbrellas.
4. He counted everything in the supply room.

Must is stronger than *should;* it usually indicates necessity.

He must finish it this week.　　She must get good grades.

D. Change these sentences so that they use verb phrases with *must*.

EXAMPLE

She saw her doctor.　　*She must see her doctor.*

1. We took the car to the garage.
2. He finished the inventory on Monday.
3. I talked to my teacher.
4. We used the money for our tuition.

Questions and negatives are formed according to the same patterns used with *will*.

> Should he see his doctor today?
> She may not finish all her work today.

The negative contracted forms in common use are *can't* (for *cannot*, written as one word), *shouldn't,* and *mustn't.*

E. Change to questions.

EXAMPLE

She can walk to work.   *Can she walk to work?*

1. He should check the oil.
2. They must take the bus to work.
3. I can leave on Thursday. (you)
4. You may talk to the teacher now. (I)
5. He should listen to the radio in his car.

F. Change to questions, using the question words indicated.

EXAMPLE

She can see her doctor on Monday. (when)   *When can she see her doctor?*

1. They must stay in a hotel. (where)
2. She can have ten days off this year. (how many)
3. He should leave for the airport at four o'clock. (what time)
4. They should come to work by car. (how)
5. I can sleep late on Sunday morning. (when) (you)

G. Change to the negative.

EXAMPLE

She can walk to work.   *She can't walk to work.*

1. He may finish the inventory on Friday.
2. They should talk in class.
3. He must park on the street.
4. You can take the packages home.
5. I can get a job this summer.

Pronunciation and Intonation Practice

A. Listen and repeat.

EXAMPLE

I must study for my exam.

1. He must finish the inventory today.
2. You must read the letters.
3. She must talk to her professor.
4. I must do my homework tonight.
5. We must get up early tomorrow.

B. Repeat several times.

ea as in *eat*	*a* as in *ate*
meet	mate
feed	fade
read	raid
seem	same

General Practice

Conversation. Your teacher will ask you to perform actions like the ones below and then ask you questions about them. Give *real* answers to the questions.

What do you need to write in your notebook?
Give your pen and pencil to _____ .
What did you do?
Can you write in your notebook now?
Put your book on _____ desk.
Where did you put your book?
Can you read your book now?
Put your notebook on the floor.
Where did you put your notebook?
Can you write in your notebook now?
Should you write in your book?
Where should you write?
Do you have any homework to do?
When should you finish it?

Reading and Oral Practice

A. Listen and repeat.

Whose birthday was it yesterday?
It was Dick's birthday.

How old was he?
He was twenty-four years old.

Did his family give him any presents?
Yes, his parents gave him a wristwatch.

What did his sister give him?
She gave him a tape recorder.

Who sent him birthday cards?
His aunt and uncle sent him birthday cards.

What did his cousins do?
They sent him cards too.

What did his friends do?
They took him out for dinner.

What did they bring him?
They brought him a compass for his car.

What did Dick show them?
He showed them his new watch.

Who else gave Dick a present?
His boss gave him a present too.

What did he give Dick?
He gave him a new job.

What is Dick's new job?
Dick will be a programmer in the accounting department.

Aunts are the sisters of one's father or mother.
Uncles are the brothers of one's father or mother.
Cousins are the children of one's aunts or uncles.
A *cousin* can be male or female.

Watch is a shortened form of *wristwatch*.

B. Answer the questions.

1. Whose birthday was it yesterday?

2. How old was he?

3. Did his family give him any presents?

4. What did his sister give him?

5. Who sent him birthday cards?

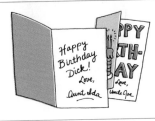

6. What did his cousins do?

7. What did his friends do?

8. What did they bring him?

9. What did Dick show them?

10. Who else gave Dick a present?

11. What did he give Dick?

12. What is Dick's new job?

C. Listen and repeat.

What do feet, inches, and yards measure?
They measure short distances.

What do centimeters and meters measure?
They also measure short distances.

How many inches are there in a foot?
There are twelve inches in a foot.

What is the plural of foot?
The plural of foot is feet.

How many feet are there in a yard?
There are three feet in a yard.

How many inches are there in a yard?
There are thirty-six inches in a yard.

How many inches are there in a meter?
There are about thirty-nine inches in a meter.

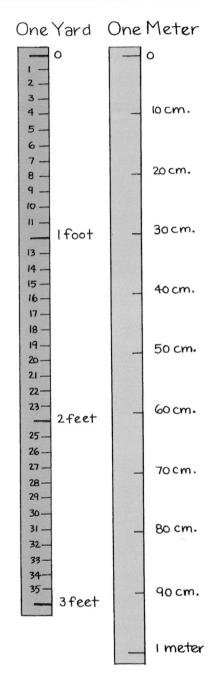

D. Answer the questions.

1. What do feet, inches, and yards measure?
2. What do centimeters and meters measure?
3. How many inches are there in a foot?
4. What is the plural of foot?
5. How many feet are there in a yard?
6. How many inches are there in a yard?
7. How many inches are there in a meter?

SALLY: Where are you going?

DICK: Downtown, and I'm in a hurry.

SALLY: I can see that. What's the matter?

DICK: I have a big date with Vanessa tonight, and I need to rent a car.

SALLY: What happened to yours?

DICK: It's in the garage for repairs. It broke down again yesterday.

SALLY: That car of yours!

DICK: Yes, I know, I should get a new one.

SALLY: Well, save your money. It's expensive to rent a car. You should try to borrow one.

DICK: I asked Bill, but he's using his this weekend. Say, what about yours?

SALLY: No, I'm sorry, I can't lend you mine. I have a lot of errands to do this evening. Did you ask Linda?

DICK: Hers is in the garage too.

SALLY: What about Diane?

DICK: She's out of town.

SALLY: Maybe she left the key with someone.

DICK: Hey, that's it! She probably left it with Tony. I'll ask him.

In English, one borrows something from someone, and lends something to someone.

>   I need to borrow an umbrella from someone.
>   Can you lend yours to me?

Broke is the past tense form of the irregular verb *to break*. *Lent* is the past tense form of the irregular verb *to lend*.

Structure and Pattern Practice

A few verbs like *to give* are followed by two objects, a direct and an indirect object. The indirect object follows the verb, and the direct object comes after it.

He lent me his car.
I wrote her a letter.
They gave him a better job.
We bought them a present.

Note that the indirect object is usually a person (or an institution) and the direct object is usually a thing.

An alternate form is a prepositional phrase beginning with *to* (or *for* in a few cases) that comes after the direct object.

He lent his typewriter to me.
I wrote a letter to her.
They gave a better job to him.
We bought a present for them.

A. Change these sentences so that they use an indirect object in place of the prepositional phrase.

EXAMPLE

I sent a card to my cousin.   *I sent my cousin a card.*

1. He showed the report to me.
2. They gave a wristwatch to Dick for his birthday.
3. I'll write a letter to you next week.
4. I made some coffee for my friend.
5. She brings the mail to her boss in the morning.
6. His sister got a tape recorder for him.
7. The mail clerk gave the stamps to us.
8. We bought a picture for you.

B. Change these sentences so that they use a prepositional phrase in place of the indirect object.

EXAMPLE

I sent my cousin a card. (to)   *I sent a card to my cousin.*

1. He wrote his uncle a letter. (to)
2. He got the boss some stamps. (for)
3. She gave the students an exam. (to)
4. He showed them the birthday cards. (to)
5. I read her the letter. (to)
6. She got him some books. (for)

C. Add the expression in parentheses.

EXAMPLE

I sent a birthday card. (my cousin)   *I sent my cousin a birthday card.*

1. She showed her notes last week. (me)
2. She read the new sentences. (to the students)
3. I'm going to lend it. (to you)
4. I showed my presents. (my cousin)

In American usage, when both the indirect and direct objects are pronouns, the prepositional phrase form is always used.

He lent it to me.   We gave it to them.

D. Change the direct and indirect objects to object pronouns and then rearrange the sentences in the correct order.

EXAMPLE

She sent her uncle the compass.   *She sent it to him.*

1. They're going to lend Dick the radio.
2. He showed Tom and me the tape recorder.
3. They showed their friends their new house.
4. He sent his sister the package.

In addition to the possessive adjectives, there are also possessive pronoun forms.

I	my	mine
you	your	yours
he	his	his
she	her	hers
it	its	
we	our	ours
they	their	theirs

My typewriter is in the repair shop. Can you lend me yours?
My schedule is very easy, but hers is very difficult.

Note that there is no possessive pronoun form for it. Also note that an apostrophe (') is not used with these forms.

E. Change the *italicized* words to the appropriate possessive pronoun.

EXAMPLE

I need to borrow your tape recorder because *my tape recorder* broke.
I need to borrow your tape recorder because mine broke.

1. We rode downtown in their car. *Our car* was in the garage.
2. My boss is in Chicago this week. *Her boss* is in Los Angeles.
3. Our school is large. *Their school* is small.
4. She talked to her teacher, but I didn't talk to *my teacher.*
5. I gave the teacher my notebook, but you didn't give her *your notebook.*
6. I found my pencil, but I didn't find *his pencil.*
7. I like our car. I don't like *their car.*
8. The books are on his desk. They aren't on *her desk.*
9. They had a party at their house, but we didn't have a party at *our house.*
10. She wrote a letter to her uncle, but I didn't write a letter to *my uncle.*

Pronunciation and Intonation Practice

A. Listen and repeat.

EXAMPLE

We gave it to them.

1. I sent it to her.
2. They showed it to me.
3. He read it to us.
4. She got them for me.
5. He lent it to me.

B. Repeat several times.

a as in *may*	*i* as in *my*
bay	by
late	light
mate	might
raid	ride
fail	file

General Practice

Conversation. Your teacher will ask you to perform actions like the ones below and then ask you questions about them. Give *real* answers to the questions.

Please give your notebook to _____ .
What did you do?
Where is his/hers? Who has yours now?
Please give _____ your pencil.
What did you do?
Where is his/hers? Who has yours now?
Please give your pen to _____ .
What did you do?
Where is his/hers? Who has yours now?
Please show _____ your book?
What did you do?
Please show your keys to _____ .
What did you do?

Reading and Oral Practice

A. Listen and repeat.

What color is the sky on a sunny day?
It's blue.

What color is the sky on a cloudy day?
It's gray.

What color is the sky at night?
It's black.

What color is grass?
It's green.

What color are carrots?
They're orange.

What color are these flowers?
They're yellow.

What color is this flower?
It's red.

What color are lemons?
They're yellow.

What color are tomatoes?
They're red.

What color is snow?
It's white.

What color is chocolate?
It's brown.

Tomato is the singular form of *tomatoes*.

B. Answer the questions.

1. What color is the sky on a sunny day?

2. What color is the sky on a cloudy day?

3. What color is the sky at night?

4. What color is grass?

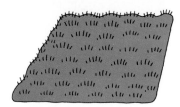

5. What color are carrots?

6. What color are these flowers?

7. What color is this flower?

8. What color are lemons?

9. What color are tomatoes?

10. What color is snow?

11. What color is chocolate?

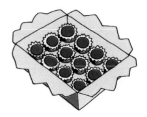

C. Listen and repeat.

Does Ron like music?
Yes, he does. He likes music very much.

Does he like classical music?
Yes, he does. He likes classical music a lot.

Does he like popular music?
Yes, he likes popular music too.

Are there any concerts at the college?
Yes, there are. There are two or three every month.

Was there a concert recently?
Yes, there was one last night.

Did Ron go to the concert?
Yes, he did. He enjoyed it very much.

Did he go alone?
No, he didn't. Sam went with him.

Did Sam enjoy the concert?
Yes, he did. He likes music too.

Are the concerts expensive?
No, they aren't. The students get a special price.

Can Ron play a musical instrument?
Yes, he can. He knows how to play the piano.

Does he play the piano well?
No, he doesn't. Music is just a hobby for him.

Is he planning to become a musician?
No, he isn't. He's planning to become a pharmacist.

To become is an irregular verb. The past tense form is *became*.

She became a doctor after many years in school.

D. Answer the questions.

1. Does Ron like music?

2. Does he like classical music?

3. Does he like popular music?

4. Are there any concerts at the college?

5. Was there a concert recently?

6. Did Ron go to the concert?

7. Did he go alone?

8. Did Sam enjoy the concert?

9. Are the concerts expensive?

10. Can Ron play a musical instrument?

11. Does he play the piano well?

12. Is he planning to become a musician?

E. Dialogue.

JOAN: Did you go shopping this evening?

SALLY: Yes, I did. They had a sale on dresses at that shop across the street.

JOAN: Did you find anything nice?

SALLY: No, I didn't. I didn't really like their clothes too much.

JOAN: What's wrong with them?

SALLY: Oh, the styles just don't suit me very well.

JOAN: Do they have a big selection?

SALLY: No, they don't. That was one of my problems. They didn't have many dresses in my size.

JOAN: What size do you wear?

SALLY: A fourteen.

JOAN: Are their clothes expensive?

SALLY: Yes, they are. There weren't any real bargains.

JOAN: Did you buy anything at all?

SALLY: Well, yes, I did. I got a scarf. Here it is.

JOAN: Oh, I like those colors!

SALLY: Yes, orange, brown, and yellow, they're autumn colors.

Clothes is a plural noun.

Her clothes are always very expensive.

The plural of *scarf* is *scarves*.

Structure and Pattern Practice

To answer *yes-no* questions in English, it is customary to use special short answer forms. Affirmative short answers consist of the word *yes* followed by the subject and the appropriate form of the auxiliary verb with which the question begins.

> *Is* he planning to become a pharmacist? Yes, he *is*.
> *Are* you going to the concert tonight? Yes, I *am*.
> *Did* he buy some records last week? Yes, he *did*.
> *Do* you like music? Yes, I *do*.
> *Can* you play the piano? Yes, I *can*.

A. Give affirmative short answers to these questions.

EXAMPLE

Is John a college student?   *Yes, he is.*

1. Are you studying English today? (I)
2. Are they waiting for the bus?
3. Is it cloudy today?
4. Is there a calendar on your desk?
5. Were you absent yesterday? (I)
6. Were there a lot of bargains in the stores?
7. Does he like to play the piano?
8. Do you copy the sentences every day? (we)
9. Did they attend the lecture?
10. Did she enjoy the concert?
11. Will she be out of town next week?
12. Will they start a new lesson next week?
13. Can you go to the concert with me? (I)
14. Should I send my cousin a birthday card? (you)
15. Will he get back on Saturday?
16. May I leave the room? (you)
17. Is your birthday in April?
18. Can she play a musical instrument?
19. Should we finish this homework now? (you)
20. Will he save some money this year?

Negative short answers consist of the word *no* followed by the subject and the negative contraction of the auxiliary used in the question.

> *Are* the concerts expensive? No, they *aren't*.
> *Does* he want to be a musician? No, he *doesn't*.
> *Should* he stay home today? No, he *shouldn't*.
> *Were* there any concerts recently? No, there *weren't*.

Note that contracted forms are not used in affirmative short answers, but that they are used in the negative. In the case of *I am*, the negative short answer is *No, I'm not*.

> Are you watching TV now? No, I'm not.

B. Give negative short answers to these questions.

EXAMPLE

Is John a computer programmer?   *No, he isn't.*

1. Are you eating an apple? (I)
2. Is she wearing a red dress?
3. Are you studying Lesson 12 today? (we)
4. Are there any students in the cafeteria now?
5. Was it sunny yesterday?
6. Was there a lot of work at the office last week?
7. Does Linda know how to play the piano?
8. Do you begin a new lesson every day? (we)
9. Did the bus stop at the corner?
10. Did you sleep late this morning? (I)
11. Did she find a lot of bargains?
12. Did his car break down again?
13. Can we leave early this afternoon? (you)
14. Can he take his vacation in July?
15. Should I miss the exam? (you)
16. Will he visit Los Angeles on this trip?
17. Is your birthday in March?
18. Will he get a job this summer?
19. Can we get tickets for the concert this evening? (you)
20. Should she spend all her money?

Pronunciation and Intonation Practice

A. Listen and repeat.

EXAMPLE

Is she a student?   Yes, she is.

1. Does he work in an office?   Yes, he does.
2. Are there some stamps in the desk?   Yes, there are.
3. Did they go to a concert?   Yes, they did.
4. Were there a lot of bargains?   Yes, there were.

B. Listen and repeat.

EXAMPLE

Is he a doctor?   No, he isn't.

1. Does she work in a shop?   No, she doesn't.
2. Is there some paper in the desk?   No, there isn't.
3. Did they go to a lecture?   No, they didn't.
4. Was there a lot of homework?   No, there wasn't.

General Practice

Conversation. Give *real* answers to these questions and to others like them that your teacher will ask.

What color is your book? Notebook? Pen? Pencil?
Do you have a car? What color is it?
Do you take a bus to school? What color is it?
Was it raining this morning? Is it raining now?
Were you early or late this morning?
Did your first class begin at _____ this morning?
Are there _____ students in the class?
Do you get to school at _____ every day?
Will you go home at _____ ?
Can you drive a car?

LESSON

15

FIFTEEN

REVIEW

Structure and Pattern Practice

A. Change to the future with *will*. Change *last* to *next*.

EXAMPLE

He worked in a bank last summer.   *He'll work in a bank next summer.*

1. He studied programming last year.
2. I studied accounting last year.
3. We went skiing last winter.
4. I visited my family last spring.
5. It rained last week.
6. She went to Chicago last month.

B. Change these sentences so that they use verb phrases with *can*.

EXAMPLE

He'll finish the inventory tomorrow.   *He can finish the inventory tomorrow.*

1. She'll find some real bargains at the sale.
2. She drove home alone.
3. He'll save some money this summer.
4. I sleep late every Saturday and Sunday morning.

C. Change these sentences so that they use verb phrases with *may*.

EXAMPLE

He went home early.   *He may go home early.*

1. We're going to attend the concert.
2. It happened in the spring.
3. They'll need more office supplies.
4. He made some money during the summer.

144

D. Change these sentences so that they use verb phrases with *should*.

EXAMPLE

You attended all the lectures.   *You should attend all the lectures.*

1. He's going to take the subway downtown.
2. He counted everything in the supply room.
3. She asked for extra homework.
4. You sleep eight hours every night.

E. Change these sentences so that they use verb phrases with *must*.

EXAMPLE

I talked to my professor.   *I must talk to my professor.*

1. I'm going to visit my family during my vacation.
2. He finished the inventory on Monday.
3. I left the office early today.
4. He looked at the dictionary.

F. Change to questions.

EXAMPLE

She can walk to work.   *Can she walk to work?*

1. She should study every night.
2. They must order supplies this week.
3. He'll try to visit New York on this trip.
4. You must count everything in the supply room. (I)
5. She can find some bargains at the sale.
6. He can get home on Saturday morning.

G. Change to questions, using the question words indicated.

EXAMPLE

She can see her doctor on Monday. (when)   *When can she see her doctor?*

1. You can sleep for eight hours. (how long) (we)
2. You should look for envelopes in the supply room. (where) (I)
3. They must finish the homework over the weekend. (when)
4. She should come to work by subway. (how)

H. Change to the negative.

EXAMPLE

She can walk to work.   *She can't walk to work.*

1. I'll go shopping this evening.
2. She'll find some bargains at the sale.
3. She should sign for that letter.
4. He can park near the office.
5. You must forget about the inventory.

I. Change these sentences so that they use an indirect object in place of the prepositional phrase.

EXAMPLE

I sent a birthday card to my cousin.   *I sent my cousin a birthday card.*

1. She gave extra homework to the good students.
2. She read the letter to the manager.
3. I showed my notebook to my teacher.
4. He got a present for his aunt.

J. Change these sentences so that they use a prepositional phrase in place of the indirect object.

EXAMPLE

I sent my cousin a birthday card. (to)   *I sent a birthday card to my cousin.*

1. We showed the new clerks the computer. (to)
2. She read the students the new sentences. (to)
3. I bought my aunt a book. (for)
4. She got him some envelopes. (for)

K. Change the *italicized* words to the appropriate possessive pronoun.

EXAMPLE

I need to borrow your car because *my car* broke down.
I need to borrow your car because mine broke down.

1. I can't find my pen, but I found *your pen*.
2. I lent him my car because *his car* was in the garage.
3. The teacher looked at your books, but she didn't look at *our books*.
4. I saw your house, but I didn't see *their house*.
5. I like your wristwatch, but I don't like *my wristwatch*.
6. I saw your letters, but I didn't see *her letters*.

L. Give affirmative short answers to these questions.

EXAMPLE

Is the exam difficult?   *Yes, it is.*

1. Did he meet a lot of men and women?
2. Are you waiting to see your professor? (I)
3. Can you see the chalkboard? (we)
4. Did they find the package?
5. Was there a lot of milk in the refrigerator?
6. Did you listen to the radio in your car? (I)
7. Does he like classical music?
8. Should she have a hobby?

M. Give negative short answers to these questions.

EXAMPLE

Will he get back on Saturday?   *No, he won't.*

1. Is she wearing a coat today?
2. Can he order more supplies today?
3. Did he park near the office?
4. Should he spend all his money right away?
5. Did they enjoy the concert?
6. Does she like popular music?
7. Will you take programming next year? (I)
8. Do you sleep eight hours every night? (I)

General Practice

Conversation. Give *real* answers to these questions and to others like them that your teacher will ask.

What year is it?
What's the date today?
What day of the week is tomorrow?
Can you sleep late tomorrow?
Were you early or late for school today?
What did you study last year?
What are you studying this year?
What are you going to study next year?
How many hours of class a day do you have this year?
How many will you have next year?
How many students are there in the class?
How many students are absent today?
When will you have your exams?
When will school end for the year?
What kind of sports do you like?
Can you swim?
What kind of weather do you like?
How's the weather today?
How was the weather yesterday?
Are you reading now?
Are you writing now?

Vocabulary

The following list includes the words introduced in Book 2. The number indicates the page on which the word first appears. If a word can be used as more than one part of speech, the way it is used in the book is as follows: n = noun, v = verb, aux = auxiliary verb, adj = adjective, pron = pronoun, prep = preposition, poss = possessive, interj = interjection, intens = intensifier. If a word has more than one meaning or is part of a longer word or expression, the meaning or complete expression used in the book will be in parentheses.

absent, 92
accept, 103
across, 8
again, 44
ahead, 67
air, 41
airplane, 106
airport, 116
almost, 87
along, 34
a.m., 18
angry, 117
another, 31
anybody, 92
anyone, 113
anything, 41
apartment, 2
April, 6
around, 8
as, 20
assistant, 2
at all, 14
August, 6
aunt, 122
autumn, 31
away, 15

back, 27
ball, 62
bank, 15
bargain, 140
basement, 20
beach, 27
become, 137
bed, 57
birthday, 90
block, 15

blow (v), 67
blow dryer, 117
born (to be born), 90
borrow, 127
boss, 123
break (down), 127
bring, 117
building, 2
bulb, 106
bus stop, 3
busy, 76
buy (v), 102

cafeteria, 15
can (aux v), 112
can't (cannot), 103
card, 122
careful, 113
carrot, 132
carry, 57
catch, 46
centimeter, 126
certainly, 82
change (v), 46
check (v), 41
child (children), 62
chocolate, 133
chore, 56
classical, 136
clean (v), 41
climb, 62
close (v), 117
clothes, 140
cloudy, 44
coat, 57
cold (adj), 30
cold (n), 46

company, 8
compass, 123
concert, 136
cool, 31
corner, 15
cough (v), 92
cough (n), 92
country (opposite
   of city), 77
(a) couple (of), 34
cousin, 123
crowded, 87

dance (to go dancing), 77
date (with a person), 8
date (calendar date), 70
December, 6
decide, 86
deliver, 102
department, 123
dictionary, 106
difficult, 67
direct (v), 67
dirty, 113
disco, 82
discover, 106
distance, 116
dollar, 41
down, 20
downtown, 2
dress (n), 140
dresser, 102
drink (v), 86
drink (n), 87
drugstore, 20
dryer, 20
during, 34

Irregular Verbs

Past Tense Forms of Irregular Verbs, Books 1 and 2

INFINITIVE	PAST TENSE FORM
to be (am, is, are)	was, were
to become	became
to begin	began
to blow	blew
to break	broke
to bring	brought
to buy	bought
to catch	caught
to come	came
to do	did
to drink	drank
to drive	drove
to eat	ate
to feel	felt
to find	found
to fly	flew
to forget	forgot
to get	got
to give	gave
to go	went
to have	had
to hear	heard
to know	knew
to leave	left
to lend	lent
to let	let
to make	made
to meet	met
to put	put
to read	read
to say	said
to see	saw
to sell	sold
to send	sent
to sleep	slept

INFINITIVE	PAST TENSE FORM
to spend	spent
to swim	swam
to take	took
to tell	told
to throw	threw
to understand	understood
to wear	wore
to write	wrote